D0828198

I CAN DO all things through Christ,
who strengthens me.
Phillipians 4:13

God bless!

Pastor Breed

Printed in the United States of America

First Printing, 2020

ISBN 9798600901858

BUD | My Life As I Recall It From My Canoe

BUD

My Life As I Recall It From My Canoe
By Milfred "Bud" Christenson

Contents

BUD | My Life As I Recall It From My Canoe

Dedicated to the memory of Muriel:
　　a wonderful WIFE,
　　a marvelous MOTHER,
　　a terrific TEACHER,
　　the original BRIDGE BUILDER.

Acknowledgements

Somewhere in life I learned a very meaningful proverb from Africa: "It takes a village to raise a child."

We use that proverb in prison ministry: "It takes a village to help a prisoner get a new start in life."

Here I want to acknowledge that it took a village to raise me.

Pa and Ma were my primary teachers in life. Pa taught me how to face adversity and come up smiling, time after time. Ma was my primary teacher. She taught the faith to me that became the foundation of my life. She also took the word "can't" out of my vocabulary.

Muriel helped me navigate leaving the farm. Her energy and enthusiasm were catchy from the start. What a partner!

My "Fabulous Four" children are amazing partners in life. They filled my life with joy and taught me to be a dad.

Ruth, my current wife and partner, continues the teaching process. Life is good at Horseshoe Lake because I share it with her. I'm not sure, at my age, that it is possible to get all the commas in the right place, but she is there to make corrections. I appreciate her encouragement regarding my simple piano playing.

Dr. Decker, Director of the School for Educational Change and Development at the University of Northern Colorado, recognized ability that I didn't see and turned my rehab experience into a path to a doctorate.

Bishop Wayne Weissenbuehler and Assistant Bob Berthelsen helped me become re-established as a pastor in the Lutheran church.

Iteffa Gobena and Almaz, with their three children, Dawit, Wengel and Banti, honored Muriel and me by inviting us to be part of the village that raised their children. The trust they placed in us still amazes me.

My many friends from Bosnia brought a new global dimension to my life. They give more than they receive.

I have learned that writing a book takes a "village of helpers" also.

It starts with my wife, Ruth, who patiently edited each chapter as I finished it. What a gift it is to be married to a former English teacher.

I can't thank Samir Muslic enough for all the work he's done in designing the book. An extra benefit comes my way because I get to sit next to him and learn. About halfway through the project he turned that task over to my son, Matt. He and his wife, Monica, worked through the final editing process. A great big THANK YOU to them as well.

It is a gift to have people who are willing to read and review the manuscript, principally Hana Muslic, a journalist from St. Louis.

I'm not a picture taker. Family and friends have provided the pictures that illustrate the story. The cover photo was taken by our neighbor, Nanette Merrill. The pictures of Bridges to Hope, Bud's Thrift Shoppe, and Freed for LIFE (with LIFE capitalized to signify not just our secular life but also our LIFE in Christ) were provided by Rhonda Mattingly and Kathy Herr. The picture of St. Paul Lutheran Church, Auburn, Nebraska was taken by Barb Knipe. The pictures from Brooklyn were taken by Jackie Lund. The ship was photographed from the helicopter by a ship photographer. I'm grateful to everyone who helped me illustrate the book.

Going Home

My story doesn't begin with my birth on our home place in Minnesota. It begins with the arrival of my canoe when I was discharged from the U. S. Navy.

In June 1960, our ship, the USS Tanner, was back in port in Brooklyn, New York. I was a "short timer," so every day seemed to pass very slowly. Work was much less while we were in port than when we were at sea, and that didn't help make the time pass. I remember that I was standing in the chow line waiting to eat lunch when a friend who worked in the ship's office came by and

1

casually said, "I just finished typing up your discharge papers, and as soon as they are signed, you will be free to go. That could happen as early as tomorrow morning!"

That set my heart racing. Is it really true? My discharge date was still a month away. Would he tell me if it wasn't true? Oh well, I'll just stay calm and wait and see. But I couldn't stay calm. I put in a request for liberty that afternoon, shined my black navy shoes, and went shopping for some civilian clothes. I was scheduled for discharge in July, so I would need new clothes anyway. I bought a pair of grey slacks and a teal and grey shirt. I checked on a flight to Minneapolis, but it was not wise to make travel arrangements until I had those cherished papers in my hands. I wanted to call my wife, Muriel, but decided that would have to wait until I had my papers and had scheduled a flight.

I returned to the ship with my new clothes and waited through a long night. Sleep wasn't coming, so I looked at the overhead and dreamed about what I would do when I got home. We had some very exciting plans. While in the Navy I had been a surveyor in the "Sea Bees," and I thought I might like to study engineering. But it was a lot more practical for me to finish my bachelor's degree to become a science and math teacher. Over a period of time, we had written letters back and forth, and decided we would move wherever Muriel got a teaching job and there was a college for me to attend. That turned out to be Duluth, Minnesota, so I enrolled at the University of Minnesota-Duluth. My division officer on the ship was Mr. Loy. His father, Dr. Loy, was the head of the Education Department at UMD. He and Mrs. Loy were very helpful to Muriel as she made plans to move. They helped her find a job in the Duluth school system and then helped her find an apartment near the school.

We didn't have any furniture, so it was a rather easy thing for Muriel to load up our Volkswagen Bug and head for Duluth. As I mulled over what might happen tomorrow, I resigned myself to the fact that we would have to take care of practical matters like buying a bedroom set, a kitchen set, and some living room furniture. However, I had two things on my mind that were priorities. As soon as it was practical, I wanted to buy a canoe and a piano.

The whirlwind in my mind became a whirlwind in my life as I was handed my discharge papers. I rushed to make flight arrangements. I stopped at the YMCA to change into my civilian clothes. I found a pay phone to call and tell Muriel the good news. We both found it hard to believe, but it was really happening!

When we arrived in Duluth, Dr. and Mrs. Loy invited us over for dinner and overwhelmed us with their generosity. They handed us a set of keys to a modern cabin on one lake and told us about a primitive cabin they owned on a second lake. Both were ours to use at any time. "Just let us know in advance so we are sure the space is available," he said.

Since our first apartment was furnished, it didn't take long to fulfill my dream of buying a canoe and a piano. It was a sight to behold when we bought the canoe and tied it on top of our Volkswagen Bug for the first time. A standard canoe was seventeen feet long, but we settled for a fifteen-footer. It was three feet longer than the car, but it rode very well on top. We only took it off the car when we were ready to put it in the water.

We fell in love with Jacob's Lake, the more primitive site. It was a small lake (by Minnesota standards), and the cabin was on an island only accessible by boat. Muriel's dad, Allan Brattland, was a game warden in Wadena, Minnesota, so Muriel grew up loving the great outdoors. She loved the canoe as much as I did.

Dr. Loy was a go-getter, so he and I sat down to make a plan. We studied my transcript from St. Cloud State College and decided it would be a good idea for me to jump right into summer school. I checked out some high school textbooks from the library to refresh my limited knowledge of chemistry and physics. I had previously concentrated on biology because of my love of nature, so I had to take tests to see where I needed to start. Dr. Loy recommended I work toward a "broad science" major with a minor in mathematics. He explained that smaller schools might have only one science teacher. I might have to teach Life Science, Biology, Chemistry, Physics and Algebra. Being young and energetic, I was up for the challenge.

Our new life was underway. We were proud owners of the Alumacraft Canoe that would be my pride and joy for the rest of my life!

Duluth

My canoe has always been my favorite possession. Muriel and I made good use of it during the time we were in Duluth, exploring the lakes and camping out. Our favorite place to camp was the island in the middle of Jacob's Lake. We didn't do much with the rustic cabin because we had a tent that we both preferred. One of my favorite memories of that island happened on a weekend when the weather seemed unsettled but we decided to go camping anyway. The forecast was for thunder showers, but that didn't matter to us. We loaded up our camping gear and headed for the lake. When we got there it was overcast, but the lake was fairly calm, so we pushed off from shore and started across to the island. When we were about halfway, the wind started to pick up and the rain fell softly. We both agreed that canoeing in the rain was fun. However, the wind came up and we strained to keep the canoe headed into the waves so we didn't swamp. When we finally arrived at our favorite island camping site, we found a nice smooth area for our tent just under the edge of the trees. It sloped slightly so the rain could drain away from the tent.

We set up camp and made a quick supper. All the while, we wondered if we had made a mistake in coming. The wind and the rain picked up. The thunder and lightning became more severe. We stood on the shore, soaked to the skin, enjoying the beauty of the storm, when an extra loud thunderclap hit and we both fell to the ground. We said, simultaneously, "Are you OK?" We both were fine and then it hit us. We thought of how humorous it was that we both fell to the ground for no real reason! We both started to laugh, and we laughed until we hurt.

The storm soon passed and we got a good night's sleep. By morning the lake had calmed down, we had a nice breakfast and then set out to explore the shore of the island. That afternoon we had an uneventful trip back home. We had shared a memorable experience that has lasted a lifetime.

Our stay in Duluth was much too short. With the help of Dr. Loy, my class schedule worked out very well for me,. After three quarters and two more summer sessions, I had finished my coursework for a bachelor's degree and only had student teaching left on my schedule. I was assigned to do my student teaching in two schools, West Junior High and Denfeld High School. Both schools were in West Duluth, a blue-collar area, so this farm boy fit right in.

After about three weeks of student teaching, I received a message from my supervising teachers that I would have a visit from the Superintendent of Schools in Duluth. The next day he arrived on schedule and I was nervous! I told myself to be calm and do my best. Ma always told me, "You can't do any more than your best!" The memory of her Norwegian Brogue tickles me to this day.

After class the superintendent sat down with me. I expected some sort of a critique of my teaching, but he simply said, "I have heard very good reports about you, and I'm here to offer you a position in the Duluth school system. How would you like to start teaching for a salary starting on Monday? We have an immediate opening at Woodland Junior High School." It was on the campus of the University of Minnesota, and he told me there would be a constant stream of students coming to observe for their classes.

I was very happy that I had spent four years in the U. S. Navy Sea Bees and that I had lots of experience as a leader. I taught the remainder of that year and picked up a second part-time job as the custodian of a Lutheran church in Duluth. Muriel and I had become good friends with the pastor and his wife. My job was to keep the stoker filled with coal to heat the building and keep the church clean. I did the heavy lifting and Muriel helped with dusting, changing altar cloths and washing windows.

That fall we enjoyed many beautiful outings exploring with our canoe. Then winter came, bringing the season of "hard water," and we put the canoe up in the garage to wait for spring to bring a new season of "soft water."

Our experience in the church was very exciting for us. We sang in the choir, taught Sunday school, and I served on the church council. Muriel often sang solos and I worked hard on my new piano to learn to accompany her. I had not studied piano and didn't have the ability to sight read music. I played by ear so the mechanics were easy for me once I figured out the tune. I will admit that I didn't play exactly what was on the page, but we managed to make music together.

One of the highlights of our work at the church came during the Christmas Season. The church was located on a large lot. It was a perfect spot for a live Christmas pageant. For my first attempt at putting together a pageant, we borrowed a donkey from some friends of the congregation, and Mary rode into Bethlehem in style. I kept the donkey in the garage below our apartment. It had originally been a carriage house, so there was plenty of room for a donkey stall. How much fun can a country boy have in the city?

Now that we were both teachers, we dreamed about our next move in life. We talked about having children and decided that we would like to have four. Muriel had one sister and always wished she had an older brother. We decided we would like to have two boys and two girls.

We also talked about our teaching careers and decided we would like to teach in a small town. We would buy a small farmstead where I could raise a few cattle and have a horse to ride for fun. We also talked about how nice it would be to raise our children in the country where they could belong to 4-H club and have animals to care for.

Then I threw a monkey wrench into the plans we were making. I had been captivated by watching our young pastor at work. People in the church often said to me, "You should think about becoming a pastor." They didn't know that I was already thinking about it. Then one spring night I couldn't sleep. I told Muriel I was going to sit up for a while, so I settled into an easy chair and looked out at the beauty of Lake Superior in the moonlight. I mused for hours about what it might be like to be a pastor. There were lots of reasons why it didn't seem to fit. I'm a crude country boy. I don't fit the image of what a pastor should be. I'm not good enough. I drink too much. I don't like suits.

Toward morning Muriel got up and asked, "Are you OK?" I then told her my thoughts about becoming a pastor. Her response didn't really surprise me. She said, "Oh, wow! I've always wanted to be a pastor's wife!"

We decided there was only one way for us to find out whether this was right for me and for us. We would simply have to enroll in the seminary and give it a try.

I called Northwestern Theological Seminary in the Twin Cities. We arranged a visit, and I was surprised when they turned me down. They said my science background was not adequate preparation to enter the seminary and recommended I spend two years in preparation. That didn't sit very well with us, so we went across town to visit Luther Seminary. They accepted me as a student with the understanding that I would audit some courses at Augsburg College. That was what we needed to hear. We went back to Duluth, bought a small trailer house, moved in, and headed for St. Paul and a new adventure.

Seminary

Seminary life was not what I expected. We lived off campus in a trailer park in east St. Paul. I quickly learned that I did not have the proper background for the courses that were required. Most of my classmates had taken pre-seminary courses in college. They had taken courses in New Testament, Old Testament, church history, biblical Greek, and biblical Hebrew. I, on the other hand, had taken courses in botany, zoology, astronomy, chemistry, physics, and trigonometry.

I did the best I could to play catch-up. I admit there were times I needed a drink so I could think clearly! Hennepin Avenue, with its abundance of bars, seemed like a welcome place to me. The seminary library did not. I took biblical Greek in a summer session and then biblical Hebrew the next summer. My grades in my early classes were not what I would like them to be, but as I got adjusted to the new subject matter I gradually improved.

To my surprise, I excelled in preaching, even though my first homiletics class literally made me sick. I was so nervous that I over prepared for my first preaching assignment. We had an old TV in our trailer that I used as my practice pulpit. My fear and my nerves got the best of me, and I ran to the bathroom to throw up. I had the scripture text and my sermon memorized. We preached our sermon to the class. When I finished, there was a strange hush in the chapel. I held my breath, waiting for the critique from my classmates and the professor. Nobody said anything! Finally, the professor said, "Wow! I really feel like I have been in church this morning!"

What a gift that was.

My seminary experience was hampered by my male ego— which demanded that I work to help pay the bills. It would not have been necessary, but I went looking for a job that I could fit into my schedule. After searching the ads in the newspaper, I found the perfect job. It was a part time teaching position at a Missouri Synod Lutheran High School just down the street from our trailer park. I felt confident that I could teach algebra and biology. I filled out the application and then waited for an interview. I didn't hear from them, so I stopped by one day on my way home from the seminary. The lady I spoke to made it clear to me that a "liberal" student from an ALC (American Lutheran Church) seminary could not teach biology in their school. I'm sure they were worried that the topic of evolution would come up.

The job that I did qualify for was at the Golden Age Nursing Home. I was hired to be an orderly on the intensive care men's wing. I worked from 3:00 p.m. until 11:00 p.m. every weekday afternoon, changing diapers and bedding, feeding those who couldn't feed themselves and answering the call lights. It was a job that I loved because it was natural for me to care for people.

Toward the end of the shift I could even squeeze in a little time to read my textbooks.

During my school years after I left the navy, we were practicing birth control; Muriel used "the pill." As we looked forward to a year of internship, however, we thought it was time to have our first child. It worked out perfectly for us. Muriel got pregnant and we were looking forward to a due date around the first of June. She was able to continue teaching through the end of the school year. Then time dragged on and on as we waited for the birth of our son. The doctor discussed a C-section with us, but decided to keep a close eye on things, and so we waited. Finally, Muriel told me the time had come, so we rushed to Swedish Hospital in Minneapolis. In those days, dads were not allowed in the birthing room. I walked the halls and checked at the desk to keep up with the progress. When the time finally came, Muriel presented me and the world with a bouncing baby boy. When I finally got to meet him, he was all cleaned up and dressed in his new baby clothes. He was snuggled in Mommy's arms, and Muriel had a triumphant smile on her face. She was proud of what she had accomplished with little help from me.

It very quickly became evident to me that the quality of teaching at the seminary left something to be desired. I was a teacher by training and had demonstrated that I was a pretty good one in my teaching experience in Duluth. My professors did not have an education background. Some simply sat at the front of the room and read their notes. Others rambled on about their experiences in parish ministry. I tried my best to listen and learn, but often at the end of class I had nothing written in my notebook. One day I came in to see my professor to explain that I had the flu all weekend, that I worked a lot of hours, and that I wanted him to know my paper would be a day late. He exploded in a rage and gave me a tongue lashing about how weak the younger generation was. With that he told me to get my butt out of his office. I turned in my paper and got it back with a big red 'B" for a grade, but it was crossed off and changed to a "C" because it was late. Oh well.

After two years, I had somewhat successfully completed my Junior and Middler years and it was time for internship assignments. Students didn't have any choice in where they would be assigned, so we waited for the list to appear on the bulletin board. I was assigned to First Lutheran Church in Williston, North Dakota. I am a country boy and I understood what that meant. It was generally understood that the better students who liked to wear suits would get the assignments that seemed a bit more "cushy." Some students who knew things about the church that I didn't know expressed their condolences about my assignment. I didn't understand what that was about, but I knew it had something to do with my internship supervisor in Williston. Once I arrived in Williston, it didn't take me long to learn what they were talking about.

Internship

When I arrived in Williston, I was impressed by the beautiful church. It was like a cathedral on the western plains. The congregation was also impressive. There were over 2,000 members, and most of them were in church every Sunday.

The Pastor took me into his office and told me about how he had built this congregation and about how proud he was of the building he had designed. He laid out his expectations for my internship. He was proud that I was the twenty-third intern. Each one had made his special contribution. He was sure I would do the same. One thing stands out from that first meeting. He said, "I want you to know that people in Williston believe that Lutheran, Conservative, and Republican all go together hand in glove." I was shocked and more than a bit offended. I was a liberal Democrat from Minnesota, the Democratic Farmer Labor (DFL) state. I could have said, "Oh, I'll fit right in! I'm a Norwegian from an immigrant family. I'm a conservative in the sense that I really believe in the conservation of our natural resources, and I'm a Republican because I'm a member of this wonderful republic in which we live and to which we pledge our allegiance." Actually, I didn't say anything, but I thought to myself, "There could well be trouble ahead for me." Of course, he held all the trump cards, so I knew I would have to do the best I could to stay out of trouble.

He showed me a box filled with cards of names and addresses. He said with a smile, "This is what I call my interns' rock pile." He expected me to start as soon as possible to visit the people on these cards. They were people who were highly unlikely to attend church, but he thought visiting them was a good learning experience for a young pastor. I was delighted with the challenge. I soon discovered that the people on the list were poor, some alcoholics, quite a few Native Americans, most with a limited education, and some with disabilities. They were my kind of people! It wasn't long before I arranged to bring some of them to church. Fortunately, we had a Volkswagen bus that made it practical to transport some of them. When we left the seminary, we had sold our trailer house for $2,800 and purchased a Volkswagen van for the same amount. The good news was we had no car payments to tax our limited budget.

The next challenge he laid out for me was an interesting one. Each year the intern was in charge of the sale of Christmas trees. He assured me that they were on order and would be delivered on time. My challenge was to sell all the trees, make money to prove I had a good head for business, and to place an order for next year's trees. The sale of trees was fairly easy. I enlisted the help of the high school youth, since the money we earned would go to the Youth Fund. Toward the end of the sale, when things started to slow down, I started to give trees away to my "rock-pile" friends.

15

When the pastor found out, he was not pleased. That was a black mark on my business savvy record.

As I traveled around the East Broadway area of town where most of these people lived, I discovered that the houses were in need of repair. Many doors didn't fit the opening or were barely hanging on by loose hinges. Some windows were broken and had been boarded up. I thought I had a great idea. "Why don't we create a work team and go out into the community to make repairs where needed? The youth and the Boy Scouts could be involved under the leadership of some of our skilled construction people." The Pastor called me in and gave me a tongue lashing! As it turned out, most of this property was owned by members of the congregation who would be mighty offended if they knew what I was suggesting. Once again, foot in mouth, I hobbled off.

In the midst of this chaos, I made a request to teach a class. The course I had in mind was being offered by Augsburg Publishing called, "Poverty and the Christian Conscience." The supervising pastor was not happy with the suggestion and tried to convince me that there were lots better courses to be taught, like: "The History of Norwegian Lutherans in America." He offered to be a resource for me. Then he told me the fascinating, if uninteresting, story about the development of the Norwegian Museum in Decorah, Iowa, where he had played a leadership role.

I finally got permission to teach the course I had proposed. I prepared some publicity materials, got an invitation in the church newsletter, and put an invitation in the local newspaper, something I later learned should have been approved by the pastor beforehand. To my surprise and delight, I soon had quite a large class. Several people came from other congregations, including several teachers, nurses, social workers, and even a banker who also served in the North Dakota state legislator. This brought a frown to the pastor's face, but we moved forward. It wasn't too long before someone got the idea that we should write a minimum wage law for North Dakota. I probably don't have to tell you how that went over.

Many young pastors were serving in small-town congregations and open-country parishes near Williston. Since our worship services were on the local radio station, pastors started to stop by to talk with me about my sermons and to have a social outlet when they came to town to shop. We decided to meet for coffee every Monday morning at First Lutheran Church. Fortunately, the pastor did not disapprove of that.

The internship year was a challenge for us as a couple. We had planned to have our first child sometime during the internship year when I had a small salary to support us. Our plans worked out perfectly, and Matthew was born in June, just before we moved to Williston. Muriel stayed with her parents for a couple of weeks, and then she and Matt came to join me in Williston. We had purchased a baby buggy and I soon earned the name, "the buggy intern," because we took him in the buggy wherever we went. It was not an easy year for Muriel. She loved our new baby, but she didn't like the fact that I had to work so many hours. She went stir crazy in the small efficiency apartment we were provided. The situation got progressively worse, and we had a serious conversation about giving up the pastoral ministry and going back to our original plans as teachers. I eventually learned that it was important for me to say "no" to some things at the church and stay home to do some family things. We invited young pastors from the area to bring their families to visit us. Soon they began to invite us, and we managed to work things out.

The high point of our internship year was the bus trip I planned to the International Youth Gathering in Detroit. The high-school youth conducted several fundraisers during the year, including the sale of Christmas trees. I asked Muriel if she would like to be a sponsor for the girls. She said "yes," but as the time came closer, she almost changed her mind. After all, we were planning to do the unthinkable—leave our precious little one with our friends. Matt did better than we did. Our friends reported that he was "as good as gold" while we were gone.

When I arrived back at the seminary for my senior year, my advisor only told me that my internship report was very interesting. When all was said and done, I got credit for the year of internship and didn't have to repeat it. It was also a treat to get together with other couples who had completed their internships to share war stories.

Senior Year

Our Senior year at the seminary was a bit easier than the first two years. The faculty seemed to treat us better now that we had successfully made it through our internships. My grades were somewhat better, and that gave me more confidence.

Now I really needed a job because Muriel was not planning to teach. She was very content to stay home and take care of our son. I landed an overnight job with IBM. That sounds impressive until you hear that I worked in a tape-testing lab. No skill was involved because the tape-testing machines did all the work. The machines would stop when there was a flaw in a tape, and I would correct the flaw, if possible. If not, that tape was discarded.

The final big challenge of seminary came in the senior year. Each seminarian was asked to write a paper with the title, "The Message I Will Preach." Each of us was assigned to a team of three professors. When the time came, we went in front of our team to "defend" the paper we had written and to convince them that we were ready to be ordained. That didn't go very well for me. My team was not impressed with my performance over the three years I had spent at Luther. Of course, they read the report of my intern supervising pastor, along with the paper I had written. They thought my paper was a bit too "folksy" and not very academic. I didn't collapse under their scrutiny, and that eventually led one of the members of the team to exclaim in frustration, "This young man is irrepressible!"

I went home later to look up the word and concluded that it meant something like, "This young man is unteachable!" Or perhaps it meant, "This young man can't be changed!" Anyway, through the many years since that encounter, I have concluded that he was right.

One day I received a telephone call from Tom, a representative of the Metropolitan Community Church in Minneapolis, asking if I would be willing to come and preach in their worship service on Sunday morning. It was a chance to earn twenty dollars, so of course I said, "Yes!" It was a delightful Sunday morning for us. It was a Japanese church. They shared their history with us, and it was fascinating. They had been resettled in Minneapolis after the war. The older group of members were the original members and were called the Issei. Many of them spoke very little English. Their children were called the Nisei and their grandchildren were called the Sansei. They lived in what came to be called "Dinky Town" in Minneapolis. Their homes were lovely, but very small. They had beautiful gardens around their homes.

The next day after I preached, I received another call from Tom asking if I would consider becoming their pastor for the remainder of my Senior year at seminary. Both Muriel and I were delighted. Though small, it was a steady salary that we could count on to get us through the year.

20

While serving that church, I soon learned about my prejudices. Three of my brothers had fought in the Pacific Theatre during World War II. The Japanese, or "Japs" as my brothers called them, had been the enemy. My brothers were not impressed by my new job.

Early on, I went to visit with Mr. and Mrs. Yamaguchi. He was a highly revered elder in the congregation and the chairman of the church council. "It was a dark and stormy night" as I walked along the sidewalk to find their home. My only experience with Japanese people was through watching movies. They were always depicted as dangerous people who carried curved knives hidden on their person. But when I arrived at their home and knocked on the door, I was relieved when Mrs. Yamaguchi opened the front door and said in broken English, "Welcome, Pastor, please come in. It is such a great pleasure to have you come to our home." I learned that Mr. Yamaguchi had a master's degree in Citrus Agriculture from UCLA. They had no choice when it came to being resettled, so they accepted their assignment to Minneapolis graciously. They established a hand laundry and spent the rest of their lives running that business. They were highly respected in their congregation and in the community.

The congregation was delighted to learn that I played the piano and that Muriel was a singer. Tom spent a considerable amount of time writing out the liturgy and their favorite hymns in phonetic syllables so I could lead worship in Japanese and Muriel could sing solos. We practiced trying to say things that we didn't understand, and the congregation was delighted with our attempts (and tried hard not to laugh out loud as we struggled to get it right). We were both surprised that we had enough courage to try it.

In January Muriel and I had a visit from the Senior Pastor at Trinity Lutheran Church in Brooklyn, New York. He came to an annual convocation at Luther Seminary on a mission. The church in Brooklyn was searching for a new Associate Pastor who would serve as a community minister. He had received a recommendation from the faculty. My history indicated that Brooklyn had been my home port when I was in the U. S. Navy. The seminary faculty played a major role in those days in deciding where each student would fit best. I'm certain they didn't have many places where they thought I might fit. I'm sure they were happy when this opportunity came along.

What I didn't know at that time was that Trinity was at odds with the Bishop of the Eastern District of the ALC, and with bishops across the country, for that matter. Trinity members were people who had come to America from Norway, mostly seamen and carpenters. They were strongly pietistic people with a history of "street preachers" and a knack for saying very long prayers. In fact, it seemed that they judged each other by their ability to pray out loud, the longer the better. Mrs. Syvertsen was the best of them all.

Muriel and I talked it over and agreed that we would serve wherever the Spirit led us, including Brooklyn. Of course, I was a natural for the job—a farm boy from Minnesota with a tendency to drink a bit too much at times. The Pastor left the convocation early, content that he had accomplished his mission. They wanted me there on June 1 because the congregation had given their pastor a gift for his twenty-fifth anniversary of ordination, a trip to Norway. I needed to run the show while he was away. There wasn't even time for me to be ordained. That would have to come later.

The sad part of going to Brooklyn was having to leave my canoe. There was no place to keep it at our apartment, so I put it up on a homemade stand at Grandpa and Grandma Brattland's in Wadena, Minnesota.

At Home in Brooklyn

There was a complication, as there usually is, before we moved to New York. Muriel and I had decided that we would not have any more children of our own. We planned to adopt one boy and two girls. We attended a pre-adoption group session for a few weeks, and everybody there agreed that we would make wonderful adoptive parents. The group also decided that we would be a good fit for multi-racial children. We filled out the papers for our first adoption and waited to hear from Lutheran Social Services of Minnesota. When May rolled around we received the good news. Our son had been chosen and we could come down to the office to meet him. We were so excited! Finally, the magic moment came and we met the cutest little guy you could ever imagine. Dark curly hair and dark eyes. What a delight! We named him Jonathan Mark.

There were complications with the adoption idea in our families. They wondered, "Why adopt? You can surely have more children if you try!" We were happy to keep trying, but we had made arrangements so we wouldn't get pregnant again. Lots of children were available for adoption, and the world was getting more overpopulated. We received messages from our parents cautioning us to move slowly and think it over carefully. We received a typewritten letter (they didn't even know how to type) from Muriel's parents telling us if we went forward with the adoption, we should not plan to come home. That threat turned out to be empty, as Muriel assured me it would. One day we got a call from her mother asking us to come home and bring the baby with us. We did, and in about fifteen minutes she said, "Can grandma hold him?" From that moment on we were one big happy family.

Jon's birth parents were still in high school when he was born. They placed him for adoption, and we were the lucky adoptive parents. Later, the laws in Minnesota changed to allow adoption agencies to help birth parents if they wanted to find the child they had placed for adoption. So just after Jon's 21st birthday, the agency checked with us to see if it would be permissible to give his birth parents our phone number. Of course, we said yes, and didn't think too much more about it until our phone rang one evening when I was busy preparing supper for my clan. Deb, Jon's birth mother, introduced herself and asked if she could speak with Jon. I only heard the beginning of their conversation, and then he went to the phone in the basement to continue speaking in private. I only remember the very touching comment, "Are you my Mom?" This was the first of our fairy-tale experiences with our three adopted children and their birth families.

After graduation at the end of May, I rushed off to Brooklyn to "mind the store" at Trinity while Muriel stayed at home with her parents until I was able to find an apartment for us. Looking for an apartment in Brooklyn without a car seemed an impossible

challenge for me. Fortunately, a young couple offered to help. We
found the unfurnished apartment in which we would eventually
live, but it was more than the housing allowance the congregation
was willing to pay. That was a bit of a problem. In January when
the Pastor came to the seminary, he told me my salary would be
$5,600 a year plus an appropriate allowance for an apartment. That
was a bit lower than the salary guidelines, and it explained part of
why they didn't work with the office of the Bishop in the call
process. When I received my letter of call, the salary approved by
the Church Council was $4,800 plus an allowance of $135 for an
apartment. I brought my dilemma to the leadership of the
congregation, and they said they were sorry, but if I looked harder
I should be able to find a less expensive apartment. I gave in and

decided to pay the difference out of my salary.

They didn't have an office for me at the church, but there was a small room behind the church office. I moved my small supply of books in, and it turned out to be very adequate. I went to work with my typical enthusiasm. Muriel had given me a poster that I put on the wall. It was a picture of a small plant with a message that said, "Bloom where you are planted!" That reflected her attitude to a "T."

Since we had been living in a furnished apartment in St. Paul, I went looking for a used furniture store. There was one down the street from the apartment, but it didn't look like any store I had ever seen. Furniture was piled high in a small garage-like building. I asked if they had any dining room furniture, because we didn't have any place to sit or to eat. The man said he had a nice table and chair set, and when he dug it out from under the piles of furniture I thought he was right. It was a mahogany set with two captain's chairs and four regular dining room chairs. He said the price would be $135 and that would include delivery. I was ready to buy the set when his partner said, "Wait a minute, that set comes with a buffet and a hutch." In a short while he had dug through the piles of furniture and came up with the two additional pieces. The whole set was much nicer than I ever thought I would find. Imagine my surprise when they delivered the entire set for $135! It matched my Baldwin spinet piano, the only other furniture we had in our living room-dining room combination.

The first big challenge came in just about two weeks. One of my seminary classmates was from this congregation. It was time for our class to plan our ordination services. He called to ask if I would be willing to ordain him. I explained that I wasn't even ordained myself! We worked out a plan where I would rush back to Minnesota, be ordained in my little country church, pick up my wife and two children, and get back in time to do his ordination. We managed to pull it off. We even managed to have our baby, Jon, baptized in worship on the morning of my ordination.

Muriel's reaction to the apartment, with our "new" dining room furniture, was typical of what I had learned to expect. She said, "It's wonderful! This life in the city is all new to me, and a bit scary, but I'll get used to it." Then she went to work scrubbing the furniture and the apartment, starting with the boys' room.

Community Ministry

The area around the church was called Sunset Park. It had been the home of Norwegian immigrants for many years, but the population when we arrived was nearly all Puerto Rican. The streets were lined with row houses with an alley in the back. Women hung their clothes on the line that stretched

across the alley and that ran on pulleys. Children played in the streets in front of the houses. The children soon taught me a number of games that we played with pink rubber balls, all variations on a game they called "kings."

I was eager to show Muriel around and to share with her a few things that I remembered from my military days and the few new things I had learned since arriving at Trinity. I liked the people who ran a deli near the church, and I really enjoyed the pizza that was served from a window on Fifth Avenue. The church was located on the corner of Fourth Avenue and Forty-Fifth Street, so the pizza parlor was only a block away. I was also eager to revisit a favorite place of my Navy days called Tad's Steak House, which was on Forty-second Street in Manhattan. I had gone there to enjoy an inexpensive steak with a salad, baked potato and Texas toast. But visiting there with Muriel would have to wait a while because we didn't have much money and we needed to furnish our new home.

After we got the house in order and settled into our new life in Brooklyn, Muriel got the same sickness she had experienced during internship. It's commonly called "cabin fever." We had parked our van and used the buses and subway to get around the city. Muriel played with our boys in the back alley. We were fortunate that it was a dead-end alley, so there was little traffic. We soon learned that we could also take the boys for a walk under the bridge that ran across the entrance to New York Harbor to the shore, where there was some sand where our boys could play. We also learned that for one dollar we could take the tunnel across the river and play in Palisades Park on the Jersey side.

I had no job description. The senior pastor spoke about Community Ministry and Youth Ministry, but I was left to define the job for myself. I asked lots of questions of the secretary and others to learn what the previous pastor had done. I learned that his title was Youth Pastor. The addition of Community Minister came about because we had moved into the 60s and congregations were under pressure to begin to relate more closely to their neighborhoods. That was especially difficult in inner city communities like Sunset Park. I had received no training for this, so I set out to learn what I could. That led me to two conclusions: 1) I could learn a lot from the children who played in the street in front of the church, and 2) I could learn a lot from the teenagers who played basketball in the backyard of the church and in the park that was nearby. Both groups were very helpful.

Two men were very influential in my early life as a community minister.

While I was in the seminary I was captivated by the work of Cesar Chavez. He taught community organization, and I enrolled in two of his weekend courses early on in my ministry.

The other was Martin Luther King, Jr. He was always in the news during my years in the seminary and became a major contributor to my development as a pastor. His "I Have a Dream" speech (August 28, 1963) has been on the wall of my office for many years. The following excerpts stand out in my mind.

"I say to you today, my friends, so even though we face the difficulties of today and tomorrow, I still have a dream. It is a dream deeply rooted in the American Dream. I have a dream that one day this nation will rise up and live out the true meaning of its creed, "We hold these truths to be self-evident, that all men are created equal."

"...Continue to work with the faith that unearned suffering is redemptive...Go back to the slums and ghettos of our Northern cities, knowing that somehow this situation can and will be changed. Let us not wallow in the valley of despair."

"I have a dream that one day...little Black boys and little Black girls will be able to join hands with little White boys and White girls as sisters and brothers."

The children of Puerto Rican families in the neighborhood around the church lived in homes where English was a foreign language. Since I was a teacher by training, it was natural for me to visit the schools and introduce myself to the principal and some teachers. They were surprised and pleased by my visit and my interest. We talked about the challenge of teaching children who were behind when they came to school, and gradually fell further behind. It was not surprising that many of them became dropouts, and that the drug scene became very attractive to them. I took that challenge with me, and Muriel and I talked late into the night about what we could do. Perhaps we could offer English classes for the parents and remedial reading for the children. I called the national church office in Minneapolis and learned that grant money was available to assist congregations with such projects. I was promised a grant of $10,000, and the local school offered to pay a teacher to oversee the program. I had all the big pieces in place, so I took the suggestion to the church council with great excitement, seeking permission to use our building that stood empty all week.

Council meetings were a new experience for me. The Norwegian pastor and I did not sit at the council table, and I quickly learned that I only spoke when spoken to. The Senior Pastor spoke for the pastoral team. That was probably a good thing, because I would have put my foot in my mouth and only hurt myself. When my proposal came up for discussion, the room got very uncomfortable. There was much discussion about how children are hard on a building. The floors would get scuffed up, and no doubt children would write on the walls. It was implied that "these" children were especially difficult to control. Some younger council members spoke about how this was an opportunity for them to do a bit of community ministry, which is why they called me in the first place. To my surprise, they finally called for a vote and the resolution passed. The $10,000 grant was the clincher.

I very quickly put the grant proposal in the mail, which I had ready to go just in case. The check arrived in no time, and we were off and running. Later we added a summer program, using a public-school teacher as coordinator, and I recruited neighborhood youth and some college students as tutors. Both programs were successful. The church council members were right, however. The floors got scuffed and the kids occasionally wrote on the walls.

Early on in my short stay in Brooklyn, New York City had three strikes: public transportation workers, sanitation workers (garbage), and the Teachers' Union. Because of my relationship with the public schools, I was attracted to the teachers' strike. I attended public meetings and got to know the leaders on both the Union's and the Board of Education's sides. Lots of misinformation was circulating in the community, and I honestly didn't know what to believe. Then the Methodist pastor in the church near us and I decided maybe we could do something to help. After much discussion, we decided to seek a grant to hire an expert to help us and others sort out the issues. Another grant proposal, this one not approved by the church council, led to another grant. We hired a professor from Harvard to come to Brooklyn to work with us for the summer. He produced a "Street Sheet," which our neighborhood youth helped to distribute. I have no idea how much good we did, but the members and leaders of our congregation were asking, "What in the world is our 'junior' pastor doing?"

By this time I had quite a following among the neighborhood youth. The local gang members became my friends. They taught me as best they could, but I'm a slow learner. If they couldn't teach me, they did their best to protect me and keep me out of trouble. One day I received a call from a drug addict with whom I had been working. He needed to see me as soon as possible, so I agreed to meet him at a subway station in the downtown area. The kids asked where I was going, and I told them. They suggested that it sounded like a set up and that I shouldn't go. I went anyway.

34

When I got there, I quickly learned that the kids were right. It was a set up, and the addict and his friend intended to rob me. To my surprise, the kids from my neighborhood were there, and after a brief confrontation, they escorted me back to the church. By the way, a "gang" in those days was primarily organized to protect the neighborhood turf, not to promote drugs and violence as it does today.

Trip to Dallas

I have always had an interest in music. I started playing the piano "by ear" when I was a child. We had an old piano in our parlor that nobody ever played. It was never tuned, but it sounded fine to me. We were an old-fashioned farm family who both "lived to work and worked to live." There wasn't a lot of time for anything else. For the most part, the parlor was off limits except on Sundays or when company came. On other days, I had to sneak into the parlor to quietly play the piano—until I got caught. Then I was sent back to the chores that had been assigned to me. I learned to pick out tunes, and then I discovered the wonderful world of chords.

We also had an old guitar hanging on the wall in the living room that was a decoration. My older brother had purchased it but then abandoned it. I don't remember how, but I somehow got new strings for it and learned a few chords so my sister and I could sing together.

My interest in music carried into my church in Brooklyn. Our congregation had a wonderful organist/choir director. He was truly a professional musician with a teaching studio in downtown Manhattan. He directed a youth choir in our church that was amazing. They sang some pretty sophisticated music. I, on the other hand, only knew old fashioned gospel hymns and folk tunes. In our youth meetings we did a lot of singing. The young people brought their friends, and finally we got the idea to form what came to be called the "Narrows Area Folk Choir." The youth came from both Brooklyn and Staten Island. "The Narrows" referred to the entrance to the New York Harbor. It wasn't long before the youth were far beyond my ability to lead them. Fortunately, I found a friend among the young adults who was a music teacher at a school on Long Island. He volunteered to be the director and turned them into a first-class singing group. We sang small concerts in churches around the area and led singing at the Eastern District ALC youth gatherings.

The choir became quite well known, and the highlight for me was when they received an invitation to sing a noontime concert at the Lincoln Center in Manhattan. Our director was very good at "staging" their concerts. I was in the audience when I noticed a guitar lying on the steps leading to the stage. When it was time for the music to begin, I saw Jimmy, one of the young people, dressed in jeans and a t-shirt coming down the aisle. Still with his back to the auditorium, he picked up the guitar and tuned it. Everybody thought he had just wandered in off the street, and there were expressions of concern. Then he turned to the audience and played the most beautiful guitar solo I had ever heard. A hush fell over the audience and the concert was underway. When he finished, the choir rushed onto the stage from both sides and started with F. Melius Christianson's, "Beautiful Savior." Toward the end of the half hour, they got to my kind of music...folk...gospel...country. They brought the house down! The applause went on and on, and when they sang an encore, all I could do was sit there in tears. Happy, happy, happy tears.

That summer I worked with the interns from three of the other congregations in Brooklyn to plan a trip to the International Youth Gathering in Dallas, Texas. The choir made it easy for us to raise money, so I scheduled two buses and we traveled to Dallas with 86 people! I never did anything in a small way, so our trip lasted nearly two weeks. We traveled upstate to Niagara Falls, crossed over into Canada, and came back through the Sioux Locks in Upper Michigan. We stayed in churches or colleges dorms along the way, and we stopped to eat at truck stops where we could find room to park the buses and be fed in a reasonable amount of time. The Narrows Area Folk Choir made up most of the traveling group, so when everyone had been served, they stood where they were seated and sang grace...in four parts! Everyone typically stood and applauded, so they often sang something fun as an encore. I was so proud.

Many of the kids from Brooklyn had not been out of the city. They were absolutely enthralled by the clouds and were treated to an old-fashioned prairie thunderstorm. Lutheran colleges and seminaries were very kind to us, letting us stay in real dorm rooms, giving us tours of their campuses, and providing us free breakfast. Three of the kids came back to attend the colleges where we stayed: two at Dana College in Nebraska and one at Oklahoma

State University. We stayed at OSU because there were no Lutheran Colleges in Oklahoma!

We thoroughly enjoyed the youth gathering, and I planned the trip home across the south and up through the Appalachian Mountains. We had raised enough money so I could treat the group to a night in a beautiful old restored hotel in Alexandria, Louisiana. As I was inside arranging hotel room assignments, I heard police sirens. My first thought was, "Oh my, I wonder what they have done!" My fears were realized when I came out to find the police talking to my group and asking, "Who's in charge of this group?"

"That would be me, sir!" I said

Some of the kids had visited a shop near the hotel and purchased blank pistols, the kind that are used as the starting gun for races. The kids staged a gunfight from behind the pillars on the steps of the hotel! The police let the kids go but took me aside and directed a verbal barrage at me that I have never forgotten! They were kind enough to hand the guns over to me after making me promise that I would keep them in my suitcase until we got back home to Brooklyn. "Yes, sir! I promise!," I said. I'm guessing the police had a good laugh when they got back to precinct headquarters.

We were having a wonderful trip, and I was getting very tired. I was ready for these last couple of days to be over and looking forward to sleeping in my own bed. Then, one of the buses broke down. The bus driver called for a replacement and assured us that it would not take "too long" before we would be on our way. As you know, "too long" is not an exact measurement. We were totally off schedule. We would never make it to our planned supper stop, so I had to figure out how to feed this crowd. It was a small town with one small grocery store and one small Mom-and-Pop restaurant, both of which were closed. The sheriff came by to see what was happening, and I asked him if he had any idea where we could get food at this time of night. He was really a nice man. He called the grocer and the restaurant proprietor, and it wasn't "too long" before the adult sponsors and I were in the kitchen of the restaurant with the proprietor frying up hamburgers and hot dogs for 88 people. We fed the bus drivers and even offered a treat to the sheriff, but he assured us that he had food at home. At least he didn't say, "I have *better* food at home."

There was only one other small incident of concern. A young man on a motorcycle came by and offered rides to the kids. Before we knew what was happening, one of the girls jumped on the back of his bike and they were heading out of town. The only prayer I had time to pray was, "Lord, help us!" Thankfully, they were back in an instant, and I thanked the young man but told him, "We don't have time for any more rides because our supper is almost ready."

We slept that night on the floor of a church, but we were very late getting there. The lady who had volunteered to meet us was patiently waiting to hear from us. Remember, there were no cell phones in those days.

We had no other incidents on the way home, and we arrived in Brooklyn on schedule. We gave our bus driver a nice tip and sent him on his way. Parents were glad to see their children, and we were all ready to be off the bus for a few days. It wasn't "too long" before the kids were saying, "Can we do this again?"

I smiled and said, "We'll see."

Ministry on the Street

From time to time, the Senior Pastor would express his concern about what I was doing. I asked, "Are there things I should be doing that I'm not getting done?" He said, "No, but sometimes I think you are doing too much." I was doing "community ministry" in the only way I knew how.

During my stay in Brooklyn, I did a lot of funerals and quite a few weddings. Since my area of concern was "the community," I did all the funerals and weddings that came from outside the congregation. The senior pastor did all those for members, and the pastor from Norway did the ones for people who worshiped in the Norwegian worship services. We had two sanctuaries. One was on the street level. It was large enough to hold about 450 people, as I remember. The second one was in the basement. It held about 200 people and was just the right size for those who spoke Norwegian. They always called a pastor from the "old country" to serve them. The funerals and weddings I did were one of the ways I connected with the people in our neighborhood.

As my time in Brooklyn went on, I had several target groups about which I became concerned: the Puerto Ricans who lived in the immediate neighborhood, the children and youth I met on the street, the "street people," and the youth from several Lutheran churches in the area. I functioned as the conference youth pastor and was also chosen to chair the Eastern District Youth Committee. At that time, the Eastern District of the ALC included the entire northeastern corner of the United States from Maine to Pennsylvania. I planned some youth gatherings that gradually grew in size. Much of what I did centered around music because it was "the 60s," and the youth seemed to love to sing the songs everybody knew and loved: "Michael Row the Boat Ashore," "This Land is Your Land," and the like. Music was very easy because I had the help of the Narrows Area Folk Choir. Every time I walked on stage at one of our youth gatherings, the kids from Brooklyn would chant, "Pass da' Bud, Pass da' Bud," They held up a cutout of large Budweiser beer cap that they had stolen from a billboard somewhere. It was a very natural expression for them because they always left the "r" out of their words. "Pastor" easily became "Pass da'." In those days I didn't mind being associated with Budweiser.

The work I did with the people in the neighborhood centered in a concern for the children. With the help of the public school, we taught English and remedial reading. Of course, the children were also invited to Sunday School and Vacation Bible School. Another opportunity came to us through a Released-Time Education program. The New York School System released the children to come to the church on Wednesdays for the last hour of the day. We did a lot of singing and taught Bible stories using flannel-graph boards.

One time, I planned an evening on a ferryboat around Manhattan for the Eastern District youth. About 400 teenagers registered, so I decided to do something special. I called a man I had met in Minneapolis while I was in my senior year in seminary and offer him a music gig leading the singing. When I first knew him, his name was David Solberg, and he made music with John Ylvisaker (who had started seminary with our class but dropped out to concentrate on music - a decision that turned out to be a great gift to the church, as many of his songs are now in our hymnal).

David was living in lower Manhattan and devoting his time to starting an acting career. As I came to understand, he was always a day late and a dollar short in those days. On Saturday night everyone boarded the ferryboat except David. I was stuck doing the best I could to salvage the party. On Sunday evening, David called to ask, "Where are you? I'm here at the dock but there is no one here!" He later changed his name to "David Sole" and did commercials and bit parts until he gained fame and a good bit of money as Hutch on the TV show, "Starsky and Hutch."

I gradually became a friend and counselor to a number of street people. As a rule, I didn't know where they lived and didn't have any way to contact them unless they came to me. I think they came because they didn't experience any judgment from me, and I treated them like friends. I was always genuinely happy to see them and would postpone what I was doing at the time to try to deal with their concerns. That usually had something to do with drugs, alcohol, or prostitution. Most of them wanted a better life but they didn't know how to get it.

I became friends with David and Don Wilkerson of "Teen Challenge" fame because we were all working in the same neighborhood and with the same people. David was often gone on speaking tours, and Don stayed behind to mind the store. On Saturday evenings, I went out with their group of volunteers on the street to invite people to their evening worship. I was a little uncomfortable there because their theology was quite different from mine, but it put me in contact with new people. Only those who responded properly in their worship service by coming forward at their invitation were invited into their programs. The others often came to me. We had an unintended partnership of sorts.

One of the saddest realities of life in the big city was the huge number of girls who got caught in prostitution. It was almost always because they had been lured into drug use and then had a desperate need for money to buy drugs. Most of them came once to ask for help, but I never saw them again. Programs were available to help them get out of the life that had them trapped. Unfortunately, many of them had left their families and had no base of support.

One girl kept coming back, however. I was very impressed by how "normal" she seemed. Talking to her was like talking to the girl next door. She did have family, but their relationship was strained. She spoke almost casually about how she missed her mother. Somehow she knew she would be able to re-establish that relationship as soon as she got her life in order. Frankly, I didn't know how to help her because what she needed was money to get into a program. I spoke to a friend about her. My friend was a counselor for girls in a program in lower Manhattan. I was happy to hear that together they worked out a plan to help her.

I didn't see her again for a couple of months, but she showed up for my going-away gathering at Trinity. I was so pleased to see her! It's an overused expression, but "it made my day." This young lady made that night a "night to remember" in the very best sense of the word. She expressed her thoughts and feelings in poetry that I'm happy to share now:

Dedicated to the Pastor on the Street—Pastor Bud

A special "thanks" to the man who gave me the strength I needed,
the will to find myself;
a comrade in Christ;
a brother in love,
Pastor Bud.

To give of myself to all I can is life to me,
To laugh with all; to weep with many;
To hold a hand; to quell an angry tongue,
Is what my place in life should be—
It takes years to sort out the angry, hostile
Emotions born in each one—
But my prayer for me—my tomorrow's
Strength shall come from the experiences of today.

* * *

Dear Lord, you committed me to live on
This earth, to breathe your air, and live your life—

You have given me the mind to question,
The heart to help,
The will to do better.
I am weak and prone to stray,
And need your guidance every day.
You have given me the gift to create verse,
Feelings never spoken from the heart.
Oh Lord, if I am to live your way,
Give me the courage to face myself,
Lest I fail to know my brother.
You've blessed an unworthy creature with a priceless gift.
Let this treasure never be forgotten.
My inspirations are short-lived.
Oh, please, give me comrades whose strength
I can draw from and they from me.
I am young, but yet am old.
I have seen life.
But have not lived long.
These days have been placed in my care.
Let me be worthy of the life you give me."

* * *

"To transcend the heights of mankind and Explore the Deity of the
Gods. To illuminate with beauty—abound with love—
Amidst the turmoil, chaos and strife—
Oh, to live one day in total peace,
Where war and hatred no longer exist.
A world where young men can walk the fields
Of love, without the albatross of a gun.
To have a day where all is each other's keeper,
True harmony and brotherhood reign supreme.
But alas my friends. This perfect scheme—
Tis nothing more than a beautiful dream.

A dream, a dream, a dream for tomorrow.
Yes, that day will bring all a glorious Sun,
And at last this world will finally be One."

She shared her poetry and then left the going away party. It was very quiet in the room as most of us fought back tears. I learned later that she completed a rehabilitation program and was working to help other girls get their lives on track.

The White Bishop

When I entered the seminary in 1962, Ma was very happy. Her experience of the church was limited to the little country church where we worshiped every Sunday as a family. So, she naturally thought I would finish my education, be ordained, and serve a similar country church. And, of course, the church would have a parsonage with a garage next door, a dining room, a white picket fence, and a back yard where children could play.

Imagine her surprise and dismay when I received my first call to serve the church in Brooklyn, New York. For her, it must have been similar to having four of her sons leave home to serve in the military. She said to me, "I know there is no place that God will send you where God won't be there ahead of you to watch over you and protect you." She was right.

The following story will illustrate both the reason for her fear and the evidence of her wisdom.

Bob was one of the "street people" who came to see me fairly regularly. We would eat pizza together and sit on one of the row-house steps and talk about life. Bob was fairly content with his life and loved to philosophize about a world where hatred would disappear and there would be peace on the streets.

On this particular weekend, I had taken a group of young adults to our church camp in the mountains. On Saturday evening, our schedule for the day was completed and I was visiting in the camp office with the camp director, a close friend of mine. Suddenly, the office door flew open and Bob stood in the doorway. He looked like a mad man. He pointed at me and said, "I'm here on a mission from God to kill you!"

I was shocked, frightened, and deeply concerned about him. The camp director took him into his office to talk and learn what had brought him to camp. He had been sitting in New York City at one of his favorite taverns having a quiet drink by himself. While he sat there thinking, he noticed that the stir sticks had chess pieces on them. He also noticed that his was a white bishop. He contemplated the white bishop for a while and concluded that this was a call from God. A voice told him that he had been chosen for a special mission. His task was to kill the "White Bishop." As he mused further, he concluded that I was the White Bishop. He set out on his mission by returning to the church to find me. The secretary told him I was at the camp and would not be back in the office until Monday morning. He picked up a camp brochure that had directions to the camp and headed for the mountains. He hitchhiked to the nearby town and then was able to hitch a ride with a delivery driver who was making a delivery at the camp.

As they talked, the camp director tried to talk him out of his mission. This only made him more agitated, however, and he finally bolted out into the night.

Later I learned that Bob had spent the entire night hiding in the woods. He covered himself with dry leaves so I would not be able to find him. He was as afraid of me as I was of him. As for me, I hid too. After visiting with the young adults I brought to camp and telling them what was happening, I spent the night trying to get some sleep on the floor of the camp office - behind locked doors.

The next morning, Bob sauntered into the dining hall as if nothing had happened. The Camp Director invited him to sit with him, and he learned at breakfast that the mission was still on. Somehow he talked Bob into going with him to town, and he promised that they would put me in the backseat of his SUV so they could keep an eye on me. We were driving along a country road at about 35 miles an hour when Bob suddenly threw open the door and did a roll into the ditch. He came up running. We both went after him and soon found him with a serious leg injury. He had jumped over a small cliff and landed on a rock that split open his leg. It was really an ugly sight; there was blood everywhere, and we could see the bone.

We dressed his wound the best we knew how, carried him back to the SUV, and proceeded to the small hospital in town that was run by some Catholic sisters. They put him into a room where a variety of instruments, including scalpels, were laid out on a shelf. I took the receptionist to one side to explain that this man was very dangerous. She tried to comfort me with the opinion that these sisters were well trained nurses and that everything would be fine. Just then Bob bolted out of the hospital with a scalpel in each hand and hobbled down the street to a nearby gas station. As luck would have it, there was a Jeep sitting in the parking area with its engine running. Bob jumped in, but the sheriff had pulled his police car behind the Jeep so Bob couldn't get out of the lot. Thankfully, someone had called the sheriff, who was wonderful. He talked very calmly with Bob and assured him that I would not be able to hurt him. He said, "I will personally protect you." His deputy arrived and, to my surprise, they were able to put a straitjacket on Bob and seat him in the police car. The sheriff told me he would handle everything from there and sent us back to camp. He promised to come back and share the outcome of all this. He made good on his promise and came back that evening as I was loading my van to head back to Brooklyn. He had taken Bob to a mental institution where his wounds were attended to and he could be retained as long as necessary.

The next morning I went to visit Bob at the hospital. He talked casually about the experience. He said things like, "That was a pretty decent roll I did out of the SUV, don't you agree? Maybe I could get a job as a stunt man. You never would have caught me if I had not hit that rock." He made it clear that he was happy to see me, and that he would soon be back in Brooklyn. There was no mention of the "White Bishop."

As it turned out, I never did see him again because I was destined to leave Brooklyn much sooner than I had planned.

Stan & Rita

One of my best friends among the street people was a very tall man of Polish decent. Stan was a heroin addict who tried hard to get off heroin by himself. I tried to convince him to go to a treatment center, but that never worked out. Like so many others, he supported his habit by stealing. Eventually he got caught, was sentenced to Edgecombe Prison, and was placed in a rehabilitation program. About once a week, I took the subway to north Harlem on Manhattan Island to visit him. He introduced me to his favorite teacher, Rita, who was a blind woman. She and her dog traveled with confidence around the city. It was all very amazing to me, but Rita was one of the happiest people I knew. She taught drama, so eventually I went to see a play that she produced.

Stan was very intelligent and took as many courses as the institution would allow. His favorites were courses like drama and art. One day he presented me with a gift. It was a painting that made me sad. It was a picture of a young woman walking away down a long, long road toward the horizon. It spoke to me about loneliness, helplessness, and hopelessness. I really wished I could convince myself that there was help ahead for her just around the corner.

Stan did very well in prison and soon earned a 24 hour leave to go home to see his Mom. She invited me over to her house when Stan came and presented me with a beautiful tea set. She didn't have much money, but she gave me something that she valued to thank me for the help I was giving her son.

It was almost time for Stan's birthday, so we invited him to our house for a birthday dinner. Muriel knew that heroin addicts liked sweets, so she put extra frosting on the cake. Our boys thought it was almost like Christmas when Muriel decorated for a birthday party and put music on the tape recorder. (We had a Wollensack recorder that I had purchased in Gibraltar on one of my Navy cruises.)

We had a nice party, but about an hour after everyone left and the boys were asleep, we discovered that our tape recorder was gone. The next morning I went to a hock shop nearby, but the recorder wasn't there. I was hoping I might be able to recover it for a price, but I wasn't that lucky. Stan was too savvy to do the obvious.

Later, I was surprised to learn that Stan and Rita had fallen in love! The next time he earned another day away from the prison, she invited him over for a steak dinner. Rita was a wonderful cook. Stan came, but he didn't stay very long after supper. When Rita had finished doing the dishes, she discovered that her paycheck was gone from her desk. She called me, heartbroken. I was heartbroken too. That week I made my usual visit to Edgecombe and confronted Stan. He cried, helplessly, as he admitted that he had taken her check and used it to buy heroin.

It is my understanding that Stan finished his time in prison and then went to college. He earned bachelor's and master's degrees and went to work as a counselor in a drug rehab center in upstate New York. I wonder, sometimes, whether I ever really forgave him for what he did to Rita. In the long run, what really matters is if he could forgive himself.

One thing I do know is this: while the experience taught Rita a good lesson about being cautious, it didn't slow her down a bit. She continued to zip around town, as she put it, with her beautiful dog by her side. What a picture. What a memory!

When I think about Rita, I also remember a man who stood on the subway every day with his cup in hand begging for handouts. His blindness got the best of him, and there didn't seem to be anything I could do about it. The serenity prayer helped me to let go: "God grant me the SERENITY to accept the things I cannot change; the COURAGE to change the things I can; and the WISDOM to know the difference."

Nancy's Adoption

The most beautiful memory I have of New York City was the adoption of our third child. We had our two boys, Matt and Jon, so now it was time to adopt the first of our girls. We went to the Lutheran Child Welfare agency to talk about adoption. There were pictures of beautiful little Black and Puerto Rican children on the subway with a caption that read, "Take two, they're small!" We only wanted one at a time. We attended some preliminary group meetings and were approved for adoption. Then we went home to wait for the agency to contact us with the name of our adoption worker.

It wasn't long before our adoption worker called and made an appointment to visit us in our home. That was really exciting, because we knew it would not be long before we had a new addition to our family. It pleased us to discover that our worker was a lovely Black woman. We had a wonderful conversation, and when she left, Muriel and I agreed we were very lucky to have her as our adoption worker. She assured us that this process would not take long because there were so many children awaiting adoption in New York.

After a couple of weeks, the adoption worker called us and apologized because the process was taking longer than she expected. Muriel asked her if there was a problem of some kind. She said, "No, but I just haven't found any children that are light enough." She was obviously referring to the color of their skin. Muriel said, "Where did that come from? That is not a concern for us." There was a long pause on the phone, and finally the adoption worker said, "Oh, I'm so sorry. I know that is not a concern of yours. I realize now that is my issue." We loved and admired her for her honesty.

It was just a few days later that we received the call inviting us to come meet the little baby girl who had been chosen for us. The plan was for us to come spend a little time with the baby, and then go back home for the night. I guess they wanted to give us time to change our minds. Like that was going to happen!

I'll never forget those first precious moments. The worker brought the baby in, all dressed up for the occasion. She handed the baby to Muriel, and I could see that this new mom was overcome with joy. The baby pushed herself away and looked at Muriel with a long, steady glance. Then all at once she settled her little head against her new mommy's breast as if to say, "You'll do just fine!"

Later, in recalling those first moments together, Muriel said, "Wow! Did you notice? I didn't choose her, she chose me!"

When we finally brought the baby home, our boys were very interested in what we had just experienced. Each of them got a turn to hold their baby sister. They both were interested in the color of her skin, and we explained that there were many Black children in New York City who needed homes. Jon made us all laugh, and we still laugh to this day when we remember his commentary. He said, "I wanted a blue one!" He was just three years old and didn't know one color from another.

One day shortly thereafter we took a ride on the Subway and showed the boys the picture of the Black and Puerto Rican babies with the caption, "Take two, they're small!" They seemed to be totally satisfied with our explanation and very proud of their baby sister.

We had spent a considerable amount of time browsing through lists of names. We agreed that choosing a name would have to wait until we saw the baby. That's exactly what we did, and when it came time to choose the name, Nancy Elise seemed perfect. It still does.

Nancy wondered about her heritage throughout her adult life, especially as it related to inheritable health issues. At age 49, she decided to use *23andMe* to learn what she could. She got more than she bargained for! She learned lots of things about her genetic make-up, and that she is mostly of west-African descent. Additionally, she and a second cousin found each other, and her second cousin wouldn't let go until she had identified Nancy's birth mother. What a wonderful story! Another fairy tale came true. Nancy told me that she and her birth mother, Gayle Brooks, talked for an hour and a half during their first call. Now they have met each other face to face. I can't wait to be included in the introductions.

We seemed to have a knack for moving shortly after we added a child to our family. During my junior (first) year in seminary, Matt was born in June. We expected to begin my year of internship in Williston, North Dakota, about the first of August. But we got a letter from the congregation to let us know that they needed us there by the first of July. They had a practice of overlapping the interns' stay by one month so the new intern could learn from the last one. I rushed off to start my internship and Muriel stayed a short time with her parents. Then she and Matt came to join me.

When Jon was adopted, we waited until the end of my senior year so that we could have some time to get acquainted with our new son before we headed for our new life in New York City. So much for the plans "of mice and men." The congregation wanted me there on the first of June. Once again I left Muriel and the boys with her parents, and I went off to work.

Now we had a new daughter and no plans to go anywhere. In fact, we had no thoughts of leaving Brooklyn at all. We were just beginning to feel comfortable in the city, and we had dreams of seeing more of the sights and sounds of this wonderful place. As it turned out, however, our stay was short.

An End and a New Beginning

When I returned from the camp in the mountains after the "White Bishop" incident, I heard a growling sound coming from the transmission of my Volkswagen van. The young adults who were on the trip were already worried about me, and now they were worried about my van. I took it to a friend who was a mechanic, and I didn't like what I heard. The transmission would have to be replaced. With our limited salary, we didn't have money for big expenses, so I was stuck without transportation. Fortunately, New York City had a great subway and bus system.

The thought occurred to me that maybe the congregation would help me since I only used my van for church related things. I went to discuss it with the Senior Pastor, but all he could do was wring his hands. He wasn't at all optimistic.

Then I took my problem to the chairman of the church council. I didn't really expect much sympathy from him, but I didn't know where else to turn. Karl was obviously disgusted with me for even asking for help. First he told me, "This is your problem, and you will have to work it out the best way you know how."

I questioned whether it might be possible for the church to help me since I used the van primarily for church-related trips. He reminded me that they had never asked me to do that. Any help I gave to the Boy Scouts, Girl Scouts, Brownies, Cub Scouts, youth group, and young adults was my choice. "Now, you will have to live with the consequences of your choices."

Then he said something that surprised me. "You are not much of a pastor. I think it is time for you to leave Trinity. So pack up your things and be on your way. Our congregation will be better off without you."

As I walked away, suddenly the gravity of the situation hit me. I didn't have any money. I didn't have a functioning vehicle. I had a wife and three small children at home in the apartment. My wife didn't know anything about these conversations I had with the Senior Pastor and the council chairman. I nearly panicked as I thought about how I was going to tell her the sad news.

As always, Muriel was wonderful. Her first concern was for me. "We will find a way," she said, "We always do. I'll call my folks, and I'm sure they will help us." That didn't make me feel any better, because I wanted them to think that I was taking care of their daughter and our kids.

Secondly, we didn't have any place to go. I had no job and she had no job. There was some comfort in knowing that we could go back to teaching if we could find a way back to Minnesota where we had teaching certificates.

I called the bishop of the Eastern District to tell him of our predicament. He was not sympathetic either. (He reminded me that Trinity and I didn't need him when they issued the call to me in the first place.) So he said, coldly, "You're on your own, buddy!" He hung up the phone with no further conversation, and I felt very much alone.

Then, a surprising sequence of events opened the door to a future. First, I remembered the name of a banker who was a member of the congregation. He wasn't very active, but he and his wife came to church occasionally. He had spoken some kind words of appreciation to me one time in the past for what I was doing in my ministry. In desperation, I called him. He invited me in for a visit. I told him our story, and he listened with obvious interest. When I finished my story, he came through with an amazing solution to my transportation problem. He told me he had a friend who sold Toyotas and asked me to take the van to him if I could. Because it wasn't very far from our apartment, I managed to limp the van over to his dealership. He and the banker arranged for a trade of my Volkswagen for a new Toyota Corolla station wagon. The banker gave me the money in the form of a low interest loan, even though I didn't have a job and didn't have any collateral.

Without any letter of resignation on my part, the leadership of the congregation started to prepare for my departure. Then, a second mysteriously wonderful thing happened. I received a telephone call from church headquarters in Minneapolis. John Schmidt, an old friend I had gotten to know at national youth gatherings, said he had been thinking about me. He thought it might be time for me to get out of the inner city and "see some babies born." Then he told me that one of his colleagues, Bob Vogel, had just accepted a call to serve as Senior Pastor at Our Savior's Lutheran Church in Denver. He said, "Bob will be needing an associate pastor to do community ministry in the Capital Hill area of downtown Denver. I hope you don't mind, but I suggested you."

Shortly after that conversation, I received a telephone call from Bob about the position they had available. Bob told me, "The work you've been doing in Brooklyn has caught the attention of lots of people in the larger church. If I was interested, Bob offered to arrange a conference call with the call committee. I heard him say, "On my recommendation, I think the committee will issue you a letter of call with just this one phone interview."

The interview was done and the letter of call was prepared and sent to the Colorado Bishop. Muriel and I thanked God for everything that was happening on our behalf and began to pack our few things for a trip across the country. We were going to have a new home in the shadow of the mountains and a "real salary" for a change. "To God be the glory," and, "I hope we are worthy of their trust!" we said to one another.

The moving van came to pick up the few things we possessed, we loaded our three kids into our new Toyota, and we headed home to Minnesota to see our parents on our way to Denver.

A New Home in Denver

The trip to Denver was very exciting for our family. It was fall and the weather was beautiful. Neither Muriel nor I had ever been to Colorado, so it was like going on vacation. Even Nebraska was new to us (an omen of things to come). I-80 was an easy drive, and we had lots of things to talk about. When we stopped at a beautiful rest stop to eat our lunch, the boys ran around like they had just been let out of confinement. The wide-open spaces were a treat for us all.

As we drove, we talked endlessly about what lay ahead of us. When we arrived, pastor Bob and his wife, Sally, offered to let us stay with them until we could find a place of our own. Their home was beautiful and spacious, and they gave us lots of tips about areas of the city we might like to choose. We were really surprised when a member of the call committee told us he didn't want us to rent. He and his wife offered to give us a personal loan for $1,200 to make a down payment on a house. He said, "Otherwise you will just waste your housing allowance and have nothing to show for it in the end."

This made Denver even more exciting for us. The day after receiving this incredibly generous offer, we wasted no time and began house hunting. We concentrated our search in the Park Hill area of Denver. This was a neighborhood that had the best house prices in town for reasons that were problematic for some. First, it was very near the airport, and the big planes flew directly overhead when they took off. That was not a problem for us. Secondly, it was a neighborhood of mixed races. That, of course, was exactly what we were looking for. In a very short time we found just the home for us. It was a poured concrete, Spanish-style house with a stucco exterior and four bedrooms. It had a back yard with a lovely cherry tree and a white picket fence, and a front yard with a grand weeping willow. The first time we saw it, the entire house was covered with vines that were turning red.

The house had not been well kept; it was a fixer-upper. That helped to make it even more affordable for us. We put in a bid for $19,000 and the owner immediately accepted. Our moving van arrived the next day with our meager belongings, so in just a couple of days we were at home in Denver. Our kids loved to roll in the grass, something they had missed out on in Brooklyn. They also loved to watch the fish in a pond in the back yard. We thought the owners were planning to come back to get the fish, but that never happened. We were not comfortable with the pond because it seemed like a real danger for the children. We were right. Summer came, Nancy had learned to walk, and one day she fell headfirst into the pool while looking at the fish. Her big brother, Matt, called for help, and we rushed out to "fish" her out of the water. It didn't take us long to empty the pool and fill it with dirt.

Early that first fall, we heard a weather forecast that made our kids very happy. The weatherman said Denver would receive four inches of snow that night. It started snowing about supper time and continued to snow throughout the night. I woke in the middle of the night and looked out to see far more than four inches. I took the garden rake and reached as high as I could to shake snow off the limbs of the trees. It turned out to be a losing battle; by morning the cherry tree had split in two. We had received not four inches, but twenty-four inches of snow. The following Sunday I told the congregation that four inches of snow was deeper in Denver than anywhere I had ever been.

Bit by bit we were able to refurbish the house so it became ours. The kitchen cabinet doors were warped and didn't shut well.

The structure of the cabinets seemed fine, so I took the doors off and replaced them with homemade plywood doors using my limited carpentry skills. When we painted them, they looked quite nice.

A nook in the kitchen had room for a kitchenette table and chair set. We didn't have one. Muriel suggested that I might build a table with benches on opposite sides. Once again, with my limited skills and her inspiration and patience, we built a breakfast nook that became one of our favorite places in the house.

We had a lovely living room with a sunken fireplace. We didn't have any furniture to put in the living room until I got an inspiration. Some old planks behind the garage had obviously been used for scaffolding. They were splattered with concrete and cracked the whole length of the plank. As it turned out, there was enough lumber for me to build us some living room furniture (after building a very sturdy "fort" for the children behind the garage). Taking my cues from the chairs popular with the "hippie communes" that had been established in some of the large old houses near our downtown church, I designed and built the chairs very low to the ground. Muriel was happy to sew some cushions for them. To this, we added a coffee table made from an old, round, oak tabletop that had been left up in the rafters of the garage and two planks crossed underneath to raise it to about a foot high. All this made our living room into a favorite gathering place for our family. We spent many a night sitting on the floor in front of the fireplace singing with my guitar, accordion, or the piano.

We had four bedrooms, two up and two down. On the first floor, Muriel and I enjoyed the master bedroom and the other was a guest room. On the second floor we had two large rooms, one for boys and one for girls. The carpets were well worn when we arrived, so we put in new carpeting throughout the house as soon as we could afford it,. We painted the boys' room blue, the girls' room pink, and we got carpet to match. With the help of some of the neighborhood youth from my youth program, we managed to install the carpet ourselves.

Our house was across the street from the local elementary school. This turned out to be a mixed blessing. The kids were really excited to have the school playground right in our front yard, but they soon learned that it was not a safe place for them. Drug dealers were everywhere in Denver, and the bigger kids stole their basketball the first time they brought it out to play. The boys always wanted me to fix things so that wouldn't happen. They were too young to understand the Serenity Prayer, "God, grant me the SERENITY to accept the things I cannot change…"

Adopting Julie

Shortly after we arrived in Denver, we began to discuss the adoption of another girl. We went to Lutheran Social Services of Colorado to begin the process. Each time we were "expecting" a new baby, we were excited. As we discussed it with our children, it was exciting for them too.

This was our third experience of adopting a child in three different states with three different agencies. Each time the process was about the same. We attended some group sessions on adoption to help us examine what it would be like to bring another child into our family. The agency worker needed time to become familiar with us and to become comfortable placing a child with us.

The family dynamics change as the family grows. I was born into a very large family with Ma and Pa and twelve children. Large farm families were common. Work on the farm shaped us as we grew. Our lives centered around the school and the country church.

Muriel grew up in a family of two children. She had one older sister. Her dad was a game warden and her mom worked at home, as most women did in those days. Their family activities centered around the two girls.

We decided we would like to have a family that fit somewhere between my large family and her small family. Four seemed like the perfect number to us. We were about to finish the beginning of our family dream. Once again we discussed possible names for our new daughter. Once again we learned that you can't really choose a name until you see the child. After completing the pre-adoption requirements, we waited for the telephone call.

The procedure was the same at each agency. We received a call to invite us to come down to meet our new child. She was a tiny little thing, almost like a small doll. We learned that her father was a Black man and her mother was Italian. She had tiny little black curls and beautiful dark eyes. Then we had to return home to contemplate this adoption. The next day we returned to take our new daughter home.

Each time we adopted a child, there was an adoption procedure that made it all legal. The children were with us and it seemed like a party to them. We celebrated with a welcoming cake that Muriel had baked and decorated.

Somewhere in the process, Matt came to his Mom and said, "I wish I could be adopted." He liked all the attention that centered around the newly adopted child. Muriel took him aside and shared with him the magical night when he was born. That seemed to help a bit.

We placed Julie's crib bed in our bedroom on the first floor. Our other children would take turns sneaking into the "nursery" to see her while she was sleeping. Muriel's mom's name was Ella so our baby became "Julie Ellen."

Julie, throughout her early life, wondered who her birth mom and dad were and what they were like. For most of her life, the laws in Colorado didn't allow the agency to help a child meet her parents. Recently, however, she was happy to learn that the laws had changed. She contacted that agency, and they gave the help she needed to find her family. It turned out to be quite easy.

She learned that her mom's name was Linda, her dad's name was Fred, and that they never married. Linda's parents did not approve of the relationship and told them Fred was not welcome in their home. Linda was a nurse, and some years after she left Colorado, she married a doctor in Florida. When she finally received the information about her birthparents, Julie's birth mom had recently died, but Julie got to view a video that depicted her life story.

The most exciting part of the discovery of her birth family was the joy of meeting her sister, Elizabeth. Liz is an engineer who lives in Austin, Texas, and travels through the country for her work. Julie went to spend some time with her and discovered they have a lot in common. They also look like their mom, and they look like each other. During one visit, Liz was showing Julie the house she was building, and one of the workers said, "It's obvious you two are sisters." They said, "Yes, and we just met!" The story was like a fairy tale.

Julie's birth father, Fred, is a well-known musician in the Denver area. Julie went to Denver to get acquainted with him and had an opportunity to sing with him during one of his shows. He came to visit us in Nebraska, and meeting him was like encountering an old friend.

Red Door Ministry

Arriving in Denver was an awe-inspiring experience for us. It was the first time we had seen the Rocky Mountains. Both Muriel and I had grown up in rural Minnesota. We were accustomed to prairies, evergreen trees, lakes and rivers, but no mountains. We loved to look west from our new home and see the majestic Rockies. We took some family trips into the foothills and dreamed about climbing Mount Evans. Eventually, we got to do some mountain hiking, but now it was time for me to go to work.

When we drove up to Our Savior's Lutheran Church, we looked for the red door on the front of the church. In the telephone interview with the call committee, I had heard them talk about the "Red Door Ministry." I had seen red doors on churches in New York and learned that it was a symbol meant to say to the world, "We are here to serve this community." Now I was called to lead the "Red Door Ministry."

I will admit I was a bit anxious. I wondered if I would be adequate to the task, but Pastor Bob and the call committee seemed to think that I was, so I fed off their confidence.

The Red Door Program had been started by Pastor Archie Madsen, who had now left Our Savior's to serve the church as Bishop of the Central District of the American Lutheran Church. Part of the intimidation I felt was because his office was just down the street.

The Red Door Ministry opened the doors of the church to the neighborhood, especially the neighborhood children. The congregation had built a lovely new addition onto the old church. The basement of the old church was turned into a recreation room with pool tables, ping pong tables, and foosball. We recruited volunteers to come play with the children and help oversee the program. Every Thursday, our congregation served a supper to the neighborhood children and youth. This was an opportunity for other ALC congregations to help out with the ministry by serving meals and participating in the fun and games. It was a great concept.

The first challenge I encountered was finding new volunteers. Some of the volunteers who had made this program a success from the beginning were burned out and ready to let someone else step in. Fortunately, two wonderful elderly women stayed on to oversee the kitchen on Thursday evenings.

I didn't know anyone! I was faced with the task of running a program for children and youth who were new to me in a building that was also new to me. I made many mistakes as I sought to get my footing, and critics were quick to point them out. But there's an old expression, "This, too, will pass," and it eventually did. Gradually, I found my way around and learned the ropes. Two things happened that opened new doors: an influx of neighborhood young adults, and a visit to the board meeting for Sky Ranch.

Sky Ranch is a summer camp belonging to the Colorado Synod of the ELCA. It is in the Rockies at an elevation over 9,000 feet at the entrance of the Roosevelt National Forest. Poudre Canyon leads the way to the camp. It is an awesome drive! When I attended my first board meeting to learn about the camp, I was surprised to learn that the camp didn't do much camping. Instead, it was run like a small midwestern camp with typical camp activities. I had just come from the Eastern District of the ALC that had an amazing camping program at Camp Koinonia in upstate New York. There, every group that came to the camp hiked through the woods to a campsite, set up camp, cooked two meals a day, and planned their own activities with the help of their counselor. I immediately started dreaming about the possibilities offered by this amazing site in the Rockies.

The chairman of the board of directors was an elderly man who had been a church bishop before retirement. He told me in no uncertain terms to keep my grandiose ideas and my enthusiasm to myself.

I couldn't forget about the mountains that surrounded the camp, so I went home to Denver dreaming about new possibilities for camping adventures. Eventually, I solicited a grant of $1,000 to purchase some tents, backpacks, and appropriate gear for backpacking. I hired two leaders from the mountaineering club at South Dakota State University and set up a camping program that Muriel and I ran out of our home. Kwen and Durand, our guides that first year, moved in with us and became part of our family. We advertised in churches around the country, and the program did well. With the money we earned, we were able to take our Red Door children and youth camping.

The second thing that happened to help me run the program was an influx of young adults who showed up to introduce themselves. Some people complained that the hippies were taking over the neighborhood. That was a good thing for me. They became a source of willing volunteers. I decided I needed to get to know them better. I set up a retreat - in the mountains of course. I developed a unique retreat format that was built around the liturgy we used for worship every Sunday.

We started with what is called the "baptism formula." I put the retreaters into small groups and asked each one to introduce himself/herself by telling us what each one knew about his/her baptism. Some were baptized Lutheran, others Roman Catholic, others not baptized at all. It was a nice way to teach about baptism.

The next retreat session was "the confession of sin." This was an opportunity to talk about "saints" and "sinners," and that we were born in sin. We had no choice in the matter. So this session became a conversation about, simply, who we are. We each talked about "what makes me who I am," and so we simply told our story to each other. It was a good way to get acquainted. Some stories were sad, some were happy. All were very important.

The next retreat session was "the confession of faith." This gave us an opportunity to talk about the God we worship. As one would guess, there were many different understandings of God. No one was judged for what he or she believed or did not believe. We learned that we were an odd assortment of Christians from a variety of denominations, as well as Jews, agnostics, and non-believers.

In our next session, we turned our attention to the "offering." We shared with each other the gifts we had to offer. We made a list of talents and strengths that, when added together, was quite impressive.

We ended our retreat with a session in which we celebrated the Lord's Supper. We offered two options: The Lord's Supper with bread and wine and the Words of Institution of our Lord, or a love feast for those who were hesitant to participate in Holy Communion.

At the beginning of each session I played the guitar and we sang appropriate folk songs. This, it turned out, was the most fun of all. Other musicians in our group promised to bring their instruments "next time we get together." They made good on their promises, and it wasn't long until we had a good singing congregation

I say "congregation" because someone suggested that we wouldn't have to wait for the next retreat to do this all again. It gradually became the format for a weekly Sunday evening worship service. We started with three small groups of 5 7 people, but everyone brought their friends, neighbors, and co-workers, and it wasn't long until we had as many as twenty small groups.

Eventually, in addition to the group who identified as Lutherans, we had groups of Roman Catholics led by a priest friend of mine, and a Jewish group led by a rabbi friend who worked in our neighborhood mental-health program. This was a bit unorthodox, to say the least, and word got to our Bishop about what we were doing. The good news is that the national church sent an informal investigator to check all of this out. He was a retired theologian, and at the end of the Sunday evening worship, he sat with tears in his eyes and said, "I've never seen anything quite like this!"

Neighborhood Friends

One very memorable experience of our family's time in Denver happened one Sunday morning after we left worship. The children wanted to go to the zoo, which was only a few blocks from our home. We decided to stop at the zoo on our way home, visit the animals until we got tired, and then eat our Sunday lunch there.

The zoo was in a neighborhood populated primarily by Black families. As such, it was natural that many of the zoo visitors that day were Black. Our daughter, Nancy, is Black, and at that time was about four years old. She surprised us by announcing that she would like to go by herself to see the animals. Muriel and I understood that to mean she was becoming aware that she was a Black child with White parents. At this early age we assumed it meant that, while she loved us and felt loved, she was a bit embarrassed when surrounded by so many Black people.

We decided to have the other children go with Muriel, and I would stay nearby in case Nancy needed me. She went off in her own direction and I stayed close. All went well until it came time for lunch. I got close enough so she could hear me and asked quietly, "What would you like to have for lunch?" She replied without looking my way, "A hot dog, chips and a grape pop." I identified a table and said, "I'll bring your food to that table and I will sit at the next table." She said, "No, Daddy, I will sit with you." We left the zoo and went home with no further mention of what had happened. It was a reminder that nothing worth doing is easy.

I'm happy to report that Nancy grew up to be a confident, talented leader in a college where she is responsible for recruiting multicultural students from around the nation. She is also a leader in the community at large and, to our delight, in the Black community. One of the many proud moments for me as a dad came when Nancy was awarded the M. Jeanne Talley Human Relations Award in 2009 by the Ohio Association for College Admission Counseling.

Many different people from the community came to visit our Red Door Program. Some came to stay and help. One such visitor was a young man who worked for the Parks and Recreation Program in Denver. His resources and my ideas and enthusiasm made a match. This enabled us to do many more things for people in the neighborhood. Our Red Door Program remained intact, however.

One day while we were playing basketball in the parking lot, a woman came to ask for help. She was moving into an apartment across the street and needed help moving some of the heavier things from the trailer to the apartment. The young people were happy to help. In the process, I learned that she was the sister of some of our regulars at Red Door. Her young 18-month-old son was sleeping under the tree in the front yard. When the moving was done, she discovered that her son was lying limp; beside him was a bottle of baby aspirins! No one knew how many he had eaten. We called 911 and he was rushed to the hospital. His mother and four brothers were hysterical, so while the medical staff worked in the emergency room, I convinced them to come with me to the chapel for prayer. They came with me but didn't stay long. I uttered a quick prayer and then followed them back to the emergency room.

When we arrived back in the ER, an alarm was sounding and the doctor and nurses were gathered around the baby's crib. "Oh, my God, he must be dying!" his mother screamed as she rushed to his side. But to everyone's surprise he was sitting up, holding his teddy bear. He was happy to see his mom. The family, to this day, declares it was a miracle and thinks I am a miracle worker. But you know and I know that, since I'm not a doctor, I did the only thing I knew how to do...pray. It had a profound effect on the whole family, but especially on the oldest brother. He and his wife became very active in the Roman Catholic Church, and eventually worked for the church in their low-income housing program.

The practice on our outdoor parking lot basketball court was for teams of three to play, and other teams of three to challenge the winner. I had some friends, young Sioux Indian men from the Indian Center, who came by every week to play basketball. One day when they came, I was playing basketball with new friends who were Navajos. I said, "Would you like to play the winners?"

They responded, "No! We will never play as long as they (the Navajos) are around." I tried my best to be a reconciler, but to no avail. I witnessed that afternoon a standard human tendency to categorize people into groups without getting to know them as individuals. It made me sad, because they were all likable young people if you took time to get to know them. It takes time to build relationships. Sometimes we won't give the time it takes, and we all lose in the end. My experience is that sometimes I may not automatically like someone, but when I take time to hear his or her story, that changes.

One day a woman from the neighborhood came in. The secretary called to tell me someone was here to see me, warning me that she looked "pretty messed up." She was an alcoholic, and as I listened to her story, I became convinced that she really wanted to change. Being an alcoholic myself, I have a pretty good idea when someone is "just blowing smoke."

It was Thursday evening, and I invited her to stay for dinner. I took her down to the recreation area to show her around, and she noticed the two women working in the kitchen. Some neighborhood children were helping as well. She immediately asked if there was something she could do. I was delighted when the women in charge of the supper put her to work with no questions asked. Red Door magic!

She continued to come by, got into out-patient treatment, and became a regular at our Sunday evening folk worship. Everyone who got to know her through the sharing sessions at our evening worship learned to like her. One Thursday evening, she was in the kitchen helping prepare supper when some people who didn't know her came by. They looked into the kitchen and one of them exclaimed, "What is SHE doing in our kitchen?" She heard the remark and quietly took her apron off and headed for the exit. We didn't see her again for some time. Then one day I met her at King Sooper's grocery store just down the street from the church. I convinced her to come in to talk with me. It took some time, but we finally convinced her that she was welcome and needed in the Red Door program. It takes time to repair damage that is done to the human spirit, but it's always worth the effort.

Another End and a New Beginning

Our family arrived in Denver in late 1969. It was a time when music played an important role in American life, not just for listening but also for participating. People loved to sing the familiar songs that everyone seemed to know. The hootenanny was a common public sing-along experience. In keeping with the practice of the day, my family changed our hair styles. Julie, Nancy and Jon wore their hair in large Afros, and Muriel, Matt and I let our hair grow long. As I look back on my experience at Our Savior's Lutheran Church, this was part of a growing separation between me and the congregation, and between my neighborhood ministry and the ministry of the congregation.

Also underway was a movement away from the hippie lifestyle. Hippies moved into the downtown Denver area and took over some of the older homes, turning them into communes. We became accustomed to the smell of marijuana. In most cases the police simply ignored the problem, if it was a problem.

As the Red Door program grew in new directions with the young adult retreats, back-packing program, and deeper connection with the Parks and Recreation Department, the congregation sensed that control was slipping away.

The newly elected president of the congregation came to visit me one day to express his dissatisfaction with what I was doing. He made it clear that there would be no raise for me this year. The reason he gave was, "The staff raises are based on merit."

In addition, the senior pastor came to visit with me about the things I was doing in the Red Door Program. From his perspective there was a problem. He said, "You seem to be having all the fun, and I seem to be doing all the work." I asked what I could do to be more helpful. He suggested that I could make some visits to the older members of the congregation. I was happy to do that, but I think the result was not all that satisfying for anyone but me. Typical of me, after a few visits, we had organized a new "Red Door" program addition with a monthly potluck for seniors. I didn't use my guitar for sing-a-longs with the seniors, but the piano worked just fine. Rather than singing the common songs of the day, we sang the old faithful gospel songs. That worked!

After a while, the senior pastor suggested that he might come some Sunday evening and preach at our Folk Service. It occurred to me that we had been worshiping for a couple of years, and he had never been to one of our worship services. I had to tell him I'd be happy to have him come and help lead the service, but that there really was no sermon. Instead, we have a rather lengthy small group Bible Study on the three weekly texts. He decided not to come.

I was too naive to realize that the time of my departure from Our Savior's was coming rather quickly. One day I got an invitation to an Executive Committee Meeting. I had never received such an invitation, so I immediately assumed I was in some kind of trouble with the leaders of the congregation. The meeting was held at the very beautiful home of the former president. There were drinks and tasty snacks of all kinds, but I didn't feel much like participating. Time dragged on, and I wondered why we weren't getting to the reason for the gathering. Finally, I said to the president, "I feel like I'm the reason for the meeting."

He said, "In a way, you are."

Before he could say more, I said, "Well, if it will be helpful, I will offer my resignation."

The senior pastor was standing nearby and responded, "Yes, that will be helpful."

I left the meeting shortly after that and headed home to tell the "news" to my wife.

A couple of days later, I was playing basketball with a few pastors when they asked me, "When is Pastor Bob leaving?"

I said, "I didn't know he was leaving."

They said, "Don't you know he has a call to become the assistant to the national bishop?"

"No," I said, "I didn't know that." I immediately blamed myself for being so preoccupied with what I was doing that I didn't know something as important as that. I realized that my resignation was important to him because my call was tied to his.

Doctoral Program

I was surprised by my wife's reaction. Muriel had been through a shock like this before when we left Brooklyn. That time she was very supportive, and we worked our way through the dilemma together and ended up in Denver. In Denver, we found the home of her dreams. She loved the Spanish style. She loved the view of the mountains. She loved the sunken fireplace in the living room. She loved the big kitchen. She loved the neighborhood.

This time she was angry. Her anger was obviously directed at me. Looking back on the events that led up to my resignation, I see things in a different light than I did at that moment. She immediately zeroed in on my drinking. A typical alcoholic, I really didn't think that it was that bad. But her response really got my attention. She said something to this effect: "Don't worry, I'll take the kids home to Minnesota, and my parents will help me raise them. But you better go out and find yourself a prostitute who 'does windows,' because you are not much of a housekeeper!"

That was totally out of character for her, but totally in keeping with the gravity of the situation. No job. No income. Deteriorating health with bleeding ulcers. I was in danger of losing everything, including my beautiful wife and wonderful children.

I turned to begging and making promises. "Please stay with me! I'll do anything you ask!"

We agreed to go to a counselor, and together we made a plan for our future. Once we got into the planning process, it was no longer just about me but about us. We needed to become better parents, so we decided to go to a parenting class…together. I liked the course so much I went back and took the training to become the teacher. We needed to work on our marriage, so we decided to go to a marriage enrichment class…together. Once again, I liked the experience so much, I went back and took the training to become a leader. I needed to find a job as soon as possible. I needed to quit drinking, and she wanted me to quit smoking also.

I started my job search with a visit to the Bishop's office to get my name into the "hopper" for a new call. I sat waiting, hoping to speak to the Bishop or one of his two associates. After a long wait in the waiting room, the secretary came to me and said, "It's not my place to tell you this, but they are not going to talk with you. The Bishop is upset with you." That surprised me a bit, but I thought, "It is what it is."

I found a minimum wage job in construction, cleaning up construction sites. Later I found a better job at Global Van Lines, moving furniture. I put my name on the list to be available at any hour of the day to help truckers load and unload their trucks. Muriel also found a job at a nearby hospital as a nurses' aide.

I couldn't afford to get into a treatment program because I needed to work lots of hours to feed my family and make the house payment. Instead, I connected with a personal growth program that centered on "marathon sessions" (twenty-four hours) and weekend classes (retreats). In the process of putting these plans together, I met Dr. Decker from the University of Northern Colorado. He took a liking to me and invited me to come for a visit with him. He invited me to enroll in The School of Educational Change and Development, which he had developed. Since I still had access to the GI Bill because I had never used it for college or seminary, I enrolled and was literally off and running on a new track.

In the next three years I occasionally asked, "What did I do to deserve this?" But I didn't sit and ponder the question too long. It was a slow process for me to decide that, "I made this mess and it's up to me to clean it up."

Dr. Decker convinced me to pursue a doctoral course. The process involved a preliminary paper that promised to lead to a doctor's degree – one that I never planned to pursue, and especially one that I never thought I would finish. Based on my experience, I contemplated how a community of people works to do good, creative things. I drew a large X representing an hourglass—with a large opening at the top and at the bottom. I let that represent a larger number of members of the community. The idea was simple: if more people were involved in the initial development of an idea, more people would buy into the project as it played out. Most ideas for the Red Door program, for example, grew out of my mind or a conversation with a very few people. Then we were saddled with the task of trying to sell it to the "many."

The initial paper also included a list of courses that I planned to take. A group of professors read the paper and returned it to me with lots of red marks and suggestions. I re-submitted it with the appropriate changes and it was approved. The course work for this program could be done anywhere, within limits. I took a couple of courses in California and some in Denver, offered by the University of Colorado. Most courses were taken on campus in Greeley, Colorado.

The second part of my program was to carry out projects to demonstrate the main thesis of the paper. I was fortunate that things fell into place for me. I had a growing sense that someone important was watching over me and opening doors. Through it all, I was gaining a new appreciation for my Higher Power.

I worked on a project with the Denver Public Schools when a new bussing program was implemented to aid in desegregation. They planned a staffing "fruit basket upset," and in many cases 80 percent of the faculty and staff of a given school would be new. We did team-building workshops to help get the faculty working together.

I also did a project with the Roman Catholic Church. An auxiliary bishop had become a friend of mine in my work in Denver. I also had a wonderful friend, Father Bert, a priest who came to Denver on Sabbatical to do some graduate work. The

Westminster Diocese and the Dodge City Diocese were short of pastors. Not enough students were entering the priesthood through the seminaries run by the diocese. I was fortunate to work with congregations that were in the process of making new plans for their futures. In some cases, this involved using more professional lay leaders. In other cases, in meant turning to the "Orders." Priests from orders such as Benedictines and Franciscans tended to be a bit more liberal than those from the diocese. Working with the congregations and their new planning teams was a delight.

Another project was a management behavior workshop with the U. S. Forest Service to help better work together creatively. We were together for a week in a motel in California. We started with some get-acquainted exercises. Two men immediately branded me a communist and left the workshop. By the end of the week we, as a group, had become good friends and the participants were about the business of trying to guess who I really was. Most of them guessed I was a priest. When I finally said I was a Lutheran Pastor, they asked if we could conclude our time together with the Lord's Supper. I spent some time talking with them about what I believe about the Sacrament, and then was given some bread and wine from the restaurant. They were all given the option to participate or not, and they all chose to do so. It was a very moving experience for them and for me, a totally unexpected one.

The time in school went by quickly because we were so very busy, and I was faced with the need to make some final plans for graduation. That meant completing my final paper followed by orals. It was the summer of 1974, and I had a full summer of classes to complete. My plan was to spend the fall semester finishing my paper and taking my orals. Because Dr. Decker and my adviser knew I was strapped for money, they arranged to allow me to register for the courses and my paper at the same time during the summer session. I could request an incomplete if necessary and finish in the fall. Saving me a quarter of tuition was very helpful. I had already completed much of the work on an initial run at my final paper, so I finished it before the summer session started and turned it in. I got it back from the readers with lots of red marks on ways I could improve.

As the summer wore on, I recovered from my initial disappointment over their response to my paper and got up early in the mornings to rewrite it. I finished it and turned it in. Guess what? They approved it, scheduled my orals, and I was finished when the summer session ended! It all seemed too good to be true. I suggested to Muriel that I really didn't want to walk through the long graduation program on a hot summer day. She would not hear of it. "We suffered through the past two and a half years just like you did, and we are going to be there to see you receive that 'hood.'"

The day of the graduation was indeed a hot summer day. Several of my friends sat with my family. To make things more interesting, several "streakers" appeared at the graduation. Afterward, we went home to cerebrate at the party that Muriel and the kids had prepared. It was a great day! Unfortunately, most of our guests knew the old me quite well, so most of my gifts were bottles of booze or six packs of Michelob. I gave them away.

Alcohol

Alcohol has played a large role in my life. Most people who know me are surprised by that statement. Like most people who have experienced a problem with alcohol or drugs, it is difficult for me to say, "I am an alcoholic." I'm writing this at age 81 and I have proven the truth of that assertion several times over the years. The celebration of my graduation was also a celebration of a temporary period of sobriety. I admit that it wasn't total sobriety, because there were occasional drinks with the people I worked with during these years.

In my growing up years we all knew Pa was totally against drinking. His preferred drink was Orange Crush. He didn't even want to drink root beer because of its name.

Like my brothers before me, I learned to drink alcohol while I was in the U. S. Navy. I was stationed on the USS Tanner, a Hydrographic Survey Ship that went out on long cruises. We typically stayed away from our home port of Brooklyn about nine months at a time. On these cruises, we got off the ship only when we were going to and coming from our destination. In the months we were working, the Executive Officer would arrange for 60 men at a time to go ashore on a deserted island with several cases of beer, volleyball equipment, and scuba diving gear.

My shipmates would not think of me as an alcoholic, but looking back from this vantage point, I know I was. Very few people ever saw me drunk. However, a typical night out on liberty would find me starting out with my friends and then leaving them to go in my own direction. They would go back to the ship, and I would get back much later. The next day I would ask, "Why did you leave me?" Their reply was always the same, "We didn't leave you, you left us. We looked around and you were gone." To this day it is hard for me to explain that, but I know it is true.

Alcohol was problematic for me through my years in the seminary and on into my years in Brooklyn and Denver. As usually happens, it was a growing problem. I gradually drank more, and the consequences gradually became greater.

The person who understood all of this better than any of my friends was my dear wife. When we were visiting with friends, they would bring out the beer. I can still see Muriel tapping one finger against the back of her hand, alerting me to the fact that I could have one, and only one.

In Denver I had a drinking buddy from the neighborhood near the church. We would typically walk down the street during the quiet time before school was out and share a pitcher of beer. Change comes in small increments for good or for ill. In this case, we gradually stayed longer until I had to ask volunteers to oversee the recreation center. More people became aware of what was happening, and I was even confronted a time or two.

After we moved to Nebraska, we enjoyed going dancing at the Pla Mor Ballroom near Lincoln. There too, we danced for a while and then stopped for a Rum and Coke. Muriel always reminded me that this was a one, and only one, drink. When I wanted a second, she would push her drink my way. Then we would dance for a while and she would be ready to go home.

Once again, my dear wife was the one who was most aware and most concerned. Muriel disliked the smell of the alcohol and the smell of cigarette smoke on my clothes. On occasion, I would find clean clothes on the back step with a note, "Please change your clothes before coming in." Is it any wonder she had had enough when I gave up my job at Our Savior's Lutheran Church with no new job to replace it?

My doctoral program was a combination of rehabilitation and education. When it all began, I made a promise to my wife that I would stop drinking and smoking, and I did. I managed to leave the smoking behind fairly quickly. Muriel had a love/hate relationship with my pipe smoking. She enjoyed it around a fire on a camping trip in the mountains, but she did not enjoy it by the fireplace in our living room (we all did dumb things like smoking in our houses and offices in those days). She packed my pipes away instead of throwing them in the garbage. I had an assortment of pipes, many of them pipes that I had purchased in Turkey. Later I took a deep breath, gave them one last, long look, and threw them in the dumpster.

Smoking was one thing, but alcohol was quite another. I have learned that alcohol is a subtle deceiver. At this writing, I am 81 years old and have in my pocket an Alcoholics Anonymous (AA) chip that says X on it representing ten years of sobriety. I have finally learned that AA meetings are important, the twelve steps are important, other people are important, and this simple chip is important to maintaining my sobriety.

In the process of searching for total sobriety, I was encouraged by a caring sponsor to write a prayer. This is the prayer I wrote:

Lord, I want to be your man today.
I want to give honor and glory to you by what I do and say;
I want to bless people along the way.
I want what I do today to have good consequences for tomorrow.
I want to learn,
I want to build,
I want to grow,
I want to become the man you created and redeemed me to be.

These days my favorite place to say that prayer is in my canoe early in the morning on Horseshoe Lake. It flows nicely into the serenity prayer:

"God, grant me the SERENITY to accept the things I cannot change;

COURAGE to change the things I can;

and WISDOM to know the difference."

Rejection

Upon completion of my doctoral program, I had a new wave of self-confidence. Surely, I thought, this will open a new future to us as a family. So, I boldly set out in search of that future.

My first stop was the Bishop's office. I still felt strongly that my calling was to continue in parish ministry. When I arrived, the Bishop and his two assistants were sitting in the coffee room with the office personnel enjoying a donut break. They greeted me cordially, if not enthusiastically, and inquired about me and my family. I responded that we were all doing quite well. Then I shared my good news. "I have completed my doctoral program and am ready to get back to work. I came to ask you to put me back on the list for the call process." My request was met with a casual "congratulations" and then an uncomfortable silence. As they got up from the table to return to their offices, one of the assistants said, "If it's that easy, we all ought to go get one," meaning, a doctor's degree.

I thought about all the late nights and long hours at the furniture moving warehouse. I thought about the toll all of this was taking on Muriel. I thought about getting up morning after morning to continue writing and re-writing my final paper. Those were the days without computers, so the paper was done on a typewriter. Making changes meant starting over on that chapter. It was not easy to dismiss an off the cuff comment from the staff at the Bishop's office without a response.

As I walked out, I thought to myself, "I didn't expect that!" I went home to share the "news" of my visit to the Bishop. This time, Muriel was totally supportive. She said, "Well, we'll just have to look somewhere else."

I proceeded to do just that. I began to network with people I knew in search of ideas. I was qualified for jobs outside of the church, so I started filling out applications. Job searches can be long and taxing, and that's what I experienced. In response to my applications, I was called in for quite a few interviews. In a couple of cases I was one of three finalists. In each case I was the only White male. In one sense it was a great time, because people were far more aware of the inequities in our society. Many organizations were about the business of making things better by hiring minorities and women. Unfortunately for me, I found myself competing for jobs as an overqualified, White male.

I returned to the Bishop's office with a request. "Could I be placed on the list of hard-to-place clergy, and would you send me to one of those national meetings?" He agreed to do that and scheduled me for a trip to Los Angeles.

Meanwhile, I had an interview for a job with the state of Nevada, one that would have us living in Carson City. Visions of

Little Joe and Hoss from the TV show Bonanza were dancing around in my head. I went there for an interview, and it went very well. It was a newly created job as a counselor for families who were in isolated areas around the state. It was a joint experiment of the Nevada School System and the State Mental Health System. They explained that I would be chauffeured by helicopter. "Wow! Is this exciting, or what!" They treated me very well, giving me a car, a temporary credit card, and a nice place to stay for a couple of days. They invited me to visit the area and get acquainted with Carson City. I did and began to check out the housing market. I even found a lovely home that would have been perfect for my family. It, like many homes in the area, had a nice horse stable, some livestock pens, and a small riding area.

At the end of my time there, they offered me the job. I raced home, in my mind at least, to share the news with Muriel and the kids. The Director of the State Mental Health Department assured me the contract would come in a few days. After a few days of waiting, however, when I had heard nothing from Nevada, I called in to check. There was a lot of hesitation in the director's voice. He asked, "Haven't you heard anything from the governor's office?"

"No, I haven't heard a thing," I said.

He said, "Well, it is not really my place to tell you this, but the governor has eliminated the position."

CRASH!!

I was very disappointed. Muriel, of course, said, "Well it was not meant to be. Aren't you glad it happened now rather than after we moved there?" She was right and positive, as usual, but for the moment I was in no mood to be so rational.

The next adventure was my trip to Los Angeles. I got a free plane ride, a free motel, and free food. I went there to meet with a representative from each of 17 Districts of the ALC. Muriel and I had agreed before I left that we would move anywhere that I could get a call to serve.

The process began with all of the candidates waiting in their motel room to be called in for their interview. One by one, the other pastors were called into the room to be interviewed by the Bishops and Assistant Bishops. Our instructions were to make a presentation, introducing ourselves in the best light we could. They had in hand our "papers" that included our history and our Bishop's recommendation.

Other pastors ahead of me had encouraging comments as they came back from their encounters with the process. Some of them were contacted immediately for further conversation with various leaders. It looked hopeful.

Finally, my turn came. My presentation included some of the important things I felt I had accomplished in Brooklyn and in Denver. I spoke about my work on the streets of New York, my involvement in the teachers' strike, the Narrows Area Folk Choir, the rather extensive education program for Puerto Rican Children in our neighborhood, and our trip to the International Youth Gathering in Dallas with 86 Brooklyn kids. It sounded impressive to me.

Then I spoke about my work in Denver. I enjoyed talking about the Red Door Program, the neighborhood youth, the young adult retreat program, the back-packing program, our association with the Denver Parks Department, our partnership with the Gilpin Mental Health Center, and our Sunday Folk Worship with emphasis on the "Folk" rather than on the "Folk Music." Again, it sounded impressive to me.

After my presentation, there were very few questions for me. I didn't know what to make of that, but I returned to my room with some hope that something good would happen.

Nothing happened. I received no invitation for a further conversation with anyone. I flew home that afternoon with nothing good to report.

Fortunately, the newly called pastor of Our Savior's Lutheran Church in Denver felt an obligation to talk to me about what happened in Los Angeles. He was a friend of some of the District representatives who had been there for my presentation. He hated to tell me that one of them said, "I wouldn't have Bud in my

District if he paid the congregation to work here!" When he asked the obvious question, "Why?" The reply, was, "The things he talked about were too good to be true, No one accomplishes those things in just three years. Anyway, his Bishop had nothing good to say about him."

That brought me to an abrupt halt. I had very little hope that I would ever work in the church again.

Meanwhile, Muriel continued to work at the Jewish Hospital in Denver as a nurses' aide, and I continued to work for Global Van Lines. I kept my name on the list of workers who would come anytime, day or night, to help truckers load or unload their trucks. We were getting by.

The Best Christmas

Time marches on in good times and in hard times. Christmas was coming, and we were determined to make it the best Christmas possible under the circumstances. That attitude was driven by Muriel, as usual. She explained that we didn't have much money for Christmas this year, and she enlisted the help of the children in making gifts. They went to the ice cream store and asked for used containers to decorate. The store saved them for her, and she and the children made waste baskets for everyone. She found little boxes which she and the children decorated as "Treasure Boxes." We didn't have money for a turkey, but she bought hamburger and buns so I could prepare Christmas dinner on the grill, a favorite of the kids. I found a small tree in the foothills, probably illegally, and brought it home for us to decorate together. The kids had secret wrapping sessions with Mom as they prepared the obvious gifts for each other. Mom also had a few surprises that she had found at Value Village for a few pennies here and there.

Christmas Eve came and there was as much enthusiasm and excitement in our home as any other Christmas I can remember. Maybe more.

Then the phone rang. It was a call from the warehouse. A trucker needed some help unloading and re-loading his truck. Could I come? "Yes! Yes! I'll be there in a few minutes." He had miles to go before he would be home for Christmas with his family. We ran up and down the ramp to finish his load. He thanked me again and again, saying, "You are a hell of a worker!" He extended his hand with a hearty, "Merry Christmas!" He left a "tip" in my hand that I didn't look at until he drove away. I pulled it out of my pocket and stood there a moment in disbelief. It was a $100 bill! I called Muriel and said, "We can go shopping!" We did. But that's not all. My nephew, who was staying with us at the time, had been given a turkey for Christmas from his workplace and wondered if we would like to have it. He was heading home to spend Christmas with his folks in Minnesota. "Thank you, thank you, thank you!"

We bought a surprise gift for each of the children and had money for the "trimmings." What is a turkey dinner without cranberries, veggies, mashed potatoes and a Christmas pie? We had it all! We all remember that Christmas as one of the best ever.

A Call to Macon

I thought the church had forgotten about me, but the youth had not. In the summer of 1974, I received a call asking if I would be willing to be the keynote speaker and song leader at the Central District Youth Convention in Oklahoma City. I asked some of my old friends to play and sing with me, and it was a welcome reprieve getting together to do a little rehearsing. Like old times.

As the New Year started, I enrolled with the Denver Public School System to be a substitute teacher. Calls started coming in and that worked out well. I didn't enjoy substitute teaching much because kids love to have fun at the expense of the sub. The subbing jobs I liked most were the calls to teach Advanced Physics or Microbiology because these classes were populated by outstanding students who were self-motivated. I usually felt like they didn't really need me, but these kids were delightful to be around.

One day toward the end of January, I received a phone call from Bennie Dean Fritson, the Council President of a small country church in a place called Macon, Nebraska. He wanted to know if I would come there for an interview. Of course I said, "Yes!" I knew nothing about Macon so I quickly checked the books to learn what I could about Zion Lutheran Church. I learned that it was a very small rural church in South Central Nebraska.

ZION AMERICAN LUTHERAN CHURCH... MACON 84

The interview was scheduled for a Saturday evening. To look more presentable, I quickly shortened my hair to collar length instead of down my back. Muriel suggested that Matt should go along to help keep me awake on the drive.

The council arranged for us to stay at the home of a member family. A while before the interview was supposed to start, the farm wife came to me to say Bennie Dean was on the phone. He told me the man who was supposed to be their pulpit supply on Sunday morning, an ALC pastor from the neighboring town of Hildreth named Mel, had just had a heart attack. He wondered if I might be willing to preach in his place. I rushed into town to the local hospital to call on the pastor who had the heart attack. He was sitting up, smiling and very easy to visit with. He apologized for being such an inconvenience. I didn't know it at the time, but Mel and I would soon become best friends.

I got back to the church in time for our scheduled call-committee meeting. Five rancher/ farmers gathered in the small sacristy that doubled as the Pastor's Office. They wore pearl button shirts, large belt buckles and cowboy boots. This country boy felt surprisingly comfortable with them. In addition, two guests were there waiting to visit with me. To my surprise they were high school students who had attended the Youth Convention in Oklahoma City. They acted like I was an old friend and wondered if I brought my guitar with me. Of course I did. I never went anywhere without it in those days. "Our congregation loves to sing. Please, could we do some singing tomorrow morning in church?"

What could I say? "Yes, of course we can!" Make a list of songs you might like to sing.

They left and the meeting went well.

The next morning 65 people were in church. After church we had a very tasty potluck dinner, and then Matt and I headed back to Denver.

As soon as I arrived home, I gave a blow by blow account of our trip to Muriel. "But, when all is said and done," I said, "I don't think they will issue me a call." I thought my country-boy story would be over-shadowed in their minds by my recent time spent in the inner city.

Not so! Monday evening we were having supper when the phone rang. It was Bennie Dean. They were gathered at the church for a congregational meeting to discuss the possibility of issuing a call to me to be their pastor. His question took me back a little. "If we issue a call, will you come and be our pastor?"

I laughed, nervously, and said, "Just a minute, I'll be right back."

I said to Muriel and the kids, "You won't believe what he just said. 'If we issue a call to come and be our pastor, will you come?'"

Muriel processed things much faster than I did. Her response was, "Do we have any other options? Yes! Tell them you will come. I'll stay here and sell the house if necessary."

So I told him, "Yes, I will come." Then he said, "Could you be here by Ash Wednesday to start the season of Lent with us?" Ash Wednesday was February 12, only two weeks away. I learned later they had already voted unanimously to issue the call before he made the phone call.

This is not the normal process for calling a pastor. But they were a tiny congregation, hoping to issue a part-time call. They were desperate for a pastor and I was desperate for a call. I guess you could say it was a perfect match.

Life in the Country

Chaos in our lives continued. Muriel and I went to work to get our house cleaned and ready to put on the market. We arranged with a realtor to show the house. The time went by much too fast, and soon it was time for me to move to Macon to begin preparations for the Season of Lent.

I arrived in Macon with a sleeping bag, a borrowed cot and a camping stool. Someone in the congregation loaned me a small black and white TV. There was an antenna on the roof, so I could receive the local channels.

In a sense, this was all very new to me. I had been a pastor in two congregations, but I had never been alone without any office staff. There was a hand crank mimeograph machine for me to use to prepare the bulletins. I didn't know how to use it, so I asked and received some help from a teacher who was a member of the congregation. I found some things I could trace to make bulletin covers. I type quite well, so that part was not difficult.

Meanwhile, Muriel and the kids were back in Denver. The house sold quickly and for a reasonable price. It was enough money to pay off the mortgage and the remainder of my education debts, with $300 left over. We decided to use that money to buy two bicycles for the kids.

It seemed like a long time to me, but the day finally came to move the family to Macon. The farmers got together with their pick-ups and horse trailers and headed for Denver. They washed the trailers and then lined them with cardboard to protect our things from farm "residue." It was like a neighborhood party for them. The women planned a reception supper when we arrived. The farmers arrived on time for the party, but we were late.

Just as we entered Kansas, I was pulled over by the highway patrol in a small town. I was taken into custody and Muriel was left to wait and entertain the kids. Eventually, we learned that I looked like someone who was "wanted." It turned out to be a mistake, but costly to us in terms of time. The members of the congregation were left to wonder what had happened to us. They sent a search party to look for us, and we met them on the road. We explained it all, and then enjoyed a delightful welcome.

Macon quickly became home to us. If you ask our children, especially the three youngest, "Where did you grow up?" They will answer, "In Macon, Nebraska." Matt was not as excited about our move because he was a very good student and a threat to some of his classmates in Franklin Junior High and High School. One crazy memory stands out. I had purchased a Honda 360 motorcycle, thinking it would be cheap transportation for me. Matt loved to ride it, so we started to practice in preparation to take the test to get a motorcycle license. He was gathering pledges for the CROP WALK and asked if he might take the Honda over to our

112

neighbors to get a pledge. I thought, why not? The road went through the wildlife preserve; he would not be near any main roads. As he arrived at the neighbor's farm, he faced a ridge of new gravel that had not been leveled. He got off the bike and pushed it around the loose gravel. Meanwhile, the highway patrolman was sitting about a quarter mile away on the highway and became suspicious of what he was seeing, so he drove down to where Matt was. Matt got a ticket and had to appear in county court.

He was put on probation and assigned to a probation officer from Minden. It is interesting to note that both the highway patrolman and the county judge had sons in Matt's class in Franklin. Of course, nothing is secret, or private, in a small town.

The probation officer called and said he would come to meet with Matt and at least one parent. He arrived on a nice autumn day. We sat down at the kitchen table to get acquainted and to fill out some paperwork. He proceeded to ask the standard questions.

Have you been in trouble before? "No, this is the first time."

What were you doing when you were arrested? "Getting a pledge for the CROP WALK."

How are you doing in school? How are your grades? "I am a straight A student."

What activities do you participate in? "I'm active in sports, participate in horse 4-H Club, sing in the high school choir, play trumpet in band, played the lead role in the school play." The list went on and on. Finally, the probation officer said, "What am I doing here?" We all laughed and Matt asked him if he would like to shoot baskets. They did, and both Matt and I felt like we had a new friend.

Even though Muriel had to sell the house she loved in Denver, she was genuinely excited about the parsonage, which was located between the small country church on one side and the cemetery on the other. Since the small dining area had no room for our buffet, we put it on the enclosed back porch and used it for storage. The house had an unfinished cellar, which we eventually used in our ministry, especially with children, and it had an open front porch.

Our "story book" life was underway. We had a very productive apple tree between the house and the cemetery. The mulberry tree in the back yard was a real nuisance, but we learned to enjoy making mulberry-rhubarb pie. The farmer who lived across the road had a large grove of trees with several cherry trees and plum trees. Down the road to the south was a grove of trees with choke cherries and currants.

I grew up on a farm with a large garden, so I did my best to make a garden like Ma had. I spaded it up by hand and planted a strawberry bed, sweet corn, peas and carrots. The farmers teased me when they saw my sweet corn patch. I had planted the corn in hills like we did in Minnesota. They wondered if I had put a small fish in each hill for fertilizer. I had a small hand cultivator, and the hills made it easier to keep the corn clean of weeds.

I wasn't familiar with zucchini and summer squash. Needless to say, I planted far too many. The members of the church all laughed when the plants started to produce and I tried to give them away. Everyone had more than enough in their own gardens. The next year I knew I would only need one plant!

We had settled in the Garden of Eden. I thought I was the frog who had been kissed by a princess and turned into a prince. The truth is, I was being kissed by a princess. The princess was named Muriel, my dear sweet wife.

We went to visit the small country schoolhouse that was about a mile from our house. This was a reminder of home for me. I went eight years to a country school just like this one. The teacher was a delight for parents to know. The kids may have had a different opinion. When school started in the fall, a small bus came by to pick up the children. Sometimes extra children got off the bus at our house to play in the church yard after school. Early on, we put up a basketball hoop in the yard and there was lots of space to play punt, pass and kick. We had a single garage that was perfect for playing "anti-i-over."

The children loved to play "church." One day I sneaked into the back of the church while they were playing. One of them was playing pastor and the others were parishioners. When the appropriate time came for Holy Communion, they came forward and to my surprise they had found the communion wafers in the sacristy. They had not broken out the wine. I didn't say a word to anyone. I reasoned, "They could be doing a lot worse than playing church."

The next year was 1976, and plans were underway for the big national anniversary celebration. I got involved in planning the celebration, especially the music. We invited the bands and choruses from the three high schools in the county. We added the church choirs and everyone rehearsed the patriotic music. It was a great cerebration.

Meanwhile, Muriel was busy getting our family ready for us to participate in the big parade. She made lovely African dresses for our girls. They were floor-length dresses made from beautiful African fabrics. She made a Norwegian folk outfit for Matt and a Mexican folk outfit for Jon. She made an old-fashioned pioneer outfit for herself and one for me. We wanted to send the message that America is home to lots of people from lots of different places. Of course, we didn't have to look very far back to remember that we were all immigrants.

The culmination of the celebration was a huge community party hosted by the newly formed Lion's Club. I got there just in time to become a founding member. We had raised some money, moved two prison barracks in, and joined them in an "L" shape to make a Lion's Club. (These barracks, which had housed German prisoners of war, were left over from World War II.) For the dinner, we cut up some dead trees from someone's grove, and then volunteers spent the night burning firewood in the bottom of a large pit. When morning came, the men met to cut and wrap chunks of beef in cheese cloth. Then they soaked the meat in barbecue sauce and wrapped it in tin foil. Large sheets of corrugated roofing were placed in the pit on top of the bed of hot coals. The meat was placed next and another set of roofing sheets was placed on top of that to form an oven of sorts. Then the pit was filled in with dirt and the meat was left to cook slowly all day. We had never seen anything quite like it. Served with potato salad, coleslaw and baked beans, it made a tasty meal. What a memory.

Ministry in Macon

We were well into the summer before the Bishop called. He was quite upset with me. That was nothing new. He said, "What in heaven's name are you doing?" I explained that I had received a call to serve Zion Lutheran Church in rural Macon and that's what I was doing. He said, "You don't even have a call!"

As I thought back on the spring and early summer, I realized he was right.

The arrangements between me and the congregation had all been done over the phone. When the congregation council got my answer, "Yes, I'll come," they set the call papers aside and never looked at them again.

I apologized to the Bishop and reported this oversight to the council president. He filled out the papers and had them ready for signatures on Sunday morning. He sent them in to the Bishop's office and we thought everything was in order.

August came, and I thought the Bishop was not going to sign them. I would be without an official call. That would have been problematic because, without a call from a congregation, I would have been taken off the clergy roster of the ALC. Finally, an official looking envelope came from the Bishop's Office in Denver containing my Letter of Call. I was official.

As fall came, we started up the confirmation program and Sunday School. Our four children were accustomed to singing with Muriel and me, so we sang here and there in the community. When we heard the children sing in Sunday School, it occurred to us that we had the makings of a good children's choir. Muriel became the director, and we had a great time producing our first children's musical. She taught each one separately and I was amazed how well they all did with solo parts. We took the crew on a tour of county nursing homes. When the word got around, we were invited to perform the musical in Axtell at a home for disabled children. They were the favorite audience of our choir members. They responded appropriately, cheering and clapping for the hero and booing the villain. Most audiences were far less enthusiastic, but polite.

I suggested to the church council that I would like to teach the Bethel Bible Series at Zion. I explained that I would go to Madison, Wisconsin, for training to become the teacher of the Series. Then I would come back and teach twelve adults for two years. At the end of those two years, they would go out to teach. The first problem they saw was that it would cost some money to register me for the program and to send me to Madison. The second problem was that they didn't believe I could recruit that many teachers from our congregation. Then someone reasoned that this would be a good way to keep me there for at least four years. The money appeared and we were on our way.

I hand selected twelve teachers for the first class. They were wonderful students, and we had two great years of learning. When they graduated, two of the trainees recruited and taught classes to members within the congregation, and two farmers went out to teach at the local nursing homes.

The Bethel Series centered around forty "concept pictures" that were illustrated by an artist from Madison, Wisconsin. Twenty illustrated concepts were from the Old Testament and twenty from the New Testament. These were painted on large canvasses that were attached to an easel. It was an amazing sight for me to see a couple of farmers leave their fields mid-morning on a Wednesday to go teach the Biblefh! Even today it brings tears to my eyes to remember it. I did stay through the program. In fact, I taught a second set of teachers.

While I was without a call, after I finished my doctoral studies, I did some informal worship services in communities of Hispanic origin around Denver. In the process, I got to know John and Diane. They knew lots of people in the community and helped us get to know the children who came for Sunday School. When we moved to Macon, we decided it would be a good experience for those children of Hispanic origin to come to Nebraska for a farm visit. With enthusiastic support from the members of our congregation and some neighboring congregations, we made a plan to bring children from Denver to stay on farms. Our children were excited about seeing their old friends.

120

John and Diane provided transportation to the country and we recruited families to host the children. Gradually the number of families grew, and we were able to host about 120 children over a few summers. The children especially liked our hayride picnics. We loaded everyone onto hayracks and went to a small canyon nearby. The children played while the adults built a fire for roasting hotdogs and marshmallows. After a wonderful picnic supper and some tasty s'mores, we gathered around the fire for a sing-along. My old guitar got put to good use on those excursions.

During the course of my stay in Macon from 1975 to 1982, I organized a young adult program in the county and a Senior Program with the United Methodist Church in town. The Methodist Church was a small church which had a difficult time keeping a pastor. It seemed that nearly every year when June rolled around, their pastor would leave. Sometimes it would take some time to get another one. I filled in whenever they needed help during the interims.

Since the Lutheran congregation at Macon was also small, it was difficult for them to pay a pastor. I agreed to serve for far less than the salary guidelines would have suggested. I asked them if I could work for some of the farmers to supplement my salary. They thought that would be fine, and I worked for a couple of farmers when I first arrived. I learned later that they were uncomfortable having their pastor work in the fields, so that source of income came to an end.

I registered to be a substitute teacher in the local public schools, and that went well for me. I taught in several of the small-town schools within about thirty miles of Macon. One day I received a call to teach in Franklin. At the end of the day the principal called me in to ask if I would consider a longer-term assignment. They had just fired their science teacher that day. He explained that they had not been able to find a teacher, so they hired a man who had been a chemist for some time but didn't have a teaching degree. That didn't go well. I didn't ask any questions. Imagine his surprise when he asked about my credentials. I had a Broad Science Major, a Math Minor and a Doctor's Degree! He almost fell off his chair. I taught for the remainder of the fall semester, and they found a full-time teacher during the Christmas break.

As an alcoholic, I had a deep sense that my higher power was watching over me. Looking back, I'm amazed at how things seem to work out for those who love the Lord.

Muriel got her Nebraska teaching certificate and started substituting as well. It wasn't long until she, too, was offered a full-time position. She especially enjoyed her last few years as head teacher in the small town of Riverton. She got along well with the local people. One day when she had car trouble, I went to Riverton to pick her up. The chairman of the local school board came by and thanked me for sharing my wife with them. He said, "She is almost like the mayor of Riverton." With her wisdom and insight, she would have made a good mayor.

Horses

As a young boy I loved horses. Pa farmed with horses until my brothers came home from the military after World War II. Several teams took turns doing the work in the fields: Bob and Beauty, King and Queen, Prince and Star, and a young colt named Nellie. I had the privilege of watching as Pa put the harness on Nellie and team her with her mother, Beauty, to teach her how to be a team member. She was wild, but Pa was tough. We also had a horse named Babe that we rode on occasion.

When my brothers came home from the military to give farming a try, they insisted on using tractors. Pa, however, trusted the horses more than he trusted himself on the tractor, so he continued to use them during my teen years. I saved my money and bought a cow pony to ride when I was herding cattle.

When we moved to Nebraska from Denver, I hoped we might find a way to have a horse or two that I could share with my children. One day we had a community celebration in Macon, and a man there provided Shetland ponies for children to ride. He had two Shetland colts tied to a light pole in the school yard, and I learned that he was hoping to find a home for them. He sold both of them to me for thirty dollars. One was black and the other was a tan color, so the kids named them Sunshine and Shadow. We didn't have a barn, so we built a house out of straw bales so they could find shelter from the winter cold. It wasn't long before they had eaten most of their home.

Our neighbor, Gus, was a horseman. He had a world champion roping horse named Klink Chuggie that professional rodeo cowboys leased for their rodeo performances. He also raced quarter horses. Among his horses, he had an older mare that was due to have a foal in the spring. He sold the mare to me for the kids to ride, but it didn't include the very expensive colt. When the baby was born, he surprised us by giving the colt to Jon as a birthday gift. Jon, our son, named him Chuggie's Champ, and he was a wonderful horse with a gentle disposition. With the help of our friend and 4-H leader, Les Detlefsen, we managed to train Champ so Jon could ride him in 4-H competitions.

John and Sarah, a young couple in our congregation, had two other horses. Over time they lost interest, so they sold them to me for a song. Bucky was an older mare that rode like a rocking horse. She made a nice partner for Nancy. The other was a young mare named Josie that had not been broke. Again, with the help of others, we managed to train her for Matt to ride in 4-H competition. She and Matt did well in trail events in 4-H horse shows, but she never learned the art of a slow gallop.

We needed one more horse so Julie could join her siblings in 4-H. I learned of a horse that was available for sale in the town of Sutton. Jocko-Bob had been in horse 4-H for several years with his owner, who was heading for college. I went to see Jocko and liked

124

him a lot. When I rode him, he became a charger. I was a little concerned that he might be too much for Julie to handle, but they assured me that he was well trained and well behaved in the arena. To our amazement, he turned into a gentle lamb when little Julie got on his back.

One of the highlights of my stay in Macon was a visit from Ma. She came down to stay with us for a few days, and she really enjoyed watching me work the horses while the kids and Muriel were in school. When she went back home to the Senior Living Center in Montevideo, she painted a horse to look like Jocko-Bob that she later gave to me. That is still one of my prize possessions.

When it came time for us to leave Macon, we had to sell the horses. It was harder for me than for the rest of the family.

Recovery and Re-creation

Every year all pastors must fill out an annual report and turn it in to the Bishop's Office. Each year I would describe with great enthusiasm what we were doing in Macon. For most pastors, Macon, as a "job site," would be very low on the list: too small, too isolated, salary too low, little prospect for growth. Yet we were having the time of our lives. Lots of good things were happening in our ministry. I was rapidly recovering my health, and we genuinely felt like an asset to our church, our community and the region.

When the Bishop read my reports, he was suspicious that I was making things up. He sent one of his associates to check us out. He came, and his wife came with him. I was genuinely happy that I was going to have visitors, so I put on some beef stew early that morning to slow cook until noon. I baked a mulberry-rhubarb pie and some fresh dinner rolls. I also invited a couple of my church council members to stop by for a visit.

When the Bishop's assistant arrived, I took him and his wife on a tour of the area. We visited the tavern-grocery store in Macon, the Methodist Church, the Lion's Club, the country school and the blacksmith shop. That's all there was in Macon. At each place we met some very nice country folks who said all the right things about me and my family.

We returned for lunch to the parsonage, which I had cleaned thoroughly, like any good housekeeper. I think they were surprised that I was able to cook and bake.

I brought out a couple of our horses and introduced them appropriately, asking if they would like to go for a ride. They were not horse people so we released the horses and went to the church to continue our tour. The building was tiny by most standards. It had a small sanctuary with a sacristy that doubled as the pastor's office. There was also a small church basement with a kitchen out of which was served some of the best pot-luck meals I have ever eaten. I also showed them the props we were preparing for our next Children's Musical, "The Story Telling Man." I showed them the Bethel Series materials and set up the easel with the Old and New Testament paintings. They seemed impressed.

When they prepared to leave, I went to the garden and packed up some fresh vegetables for them to take with them. I laid out a painting drop cloth and shook the mulberry tree so they could have fresh mulberries. Then I gave them some fresh rhubarb so they could make mulberry-rhubarb pie. I picked apples from the apple tree and offered to take them across the road to pick cherries and plums. They declined that offer. I gathered fresh strawberries from our strawberry patch and, of course, gave them plenty of zucchini.

I learned later that they were duly impressed by their visit and said to the Bishop, "It's all TRUE! His report is all true!"

About that time I was elected "Clergy Dean" for the conference, which meant I had to attend some district meetings. The Bishop was cordial and as he got re-acquainted with the new me, he invited me to serve in several ways on committees and task forces. It was a great feeling to be back in the good graces of the Central District of the ALC.

While in recovery mode, I learned some very important life lessons. Giving up drinking and smoking was a very small beginning. Friends gave me a book entitled, "Human Life Styling." It was written by a doctor of preventive medicine with the assistance of a medical writer. The book stressed four aspects of the good life: proper diet, proper exercise, proper rest and relaxation, and involvement in things that help others.

I started running, and before long I was able to run "around the section" (four miles), then six miles and then eight. Running in local 5-K races became a new hobby. My little daughter, Julie, surprised me. She could run alongside me for miles and never stop talking. I personally found it difficult to talk and run at the same time.

I learned in running the 5-K races that my lungs were not very strong. I never did as well, or ran as fast, as I thought I should. My son, Jon, joined me in running the 5-K in Franklin. I told him, "Don't wait for me," so he ran ahead and took second in the race.

Then he turned around and ran back to meet me and finished the race a second time.

I learned that sugar was the most abused drug in the United States. The writers contrasted the things we ingested into two categories: drugs and food. Food needs to go through our digestive system. Drugs by-pass our stomach and go directly into the blood stream. Highly processed sugars qualify as drugs.

I learned that much of the food we eat is pre-digested to make it easier and faster to prepare.

I learned that it is good to eat vegetables that require some chewing, the closer to fresh the better. My children were not totally on board with what I was learning. I started to grow bean sprouts and alfalfa sprouts in the kitchen window. They got very suspicious and learned to ask, "What did you put in this, Dad?" I started to pop milo and roast soybeans for snacks; they preferred popcorn and peanuts. I started blending fruits and vegetables in various ways; they preferred Tang and Kool Aid.

Eating lower on the food chain is good for many reasons: less meat and more vegetables.

I continued to practice meditation techniques while my wife was off teaching and the children were in school. Macon was the perfect place for recovery.

After a couple of years, I decided it was time for me to have a health check-up. I had never seen such a good report card. Everything on the health chart was nicely centered; heartbeat 56, blood pressure normal, cholesterol good, no sign of ulcers. I was on the right track.

Since we didn't have very much money, we learned to do simple, inexpensive things for recreation. Camping was a family favorite. We started camping while we lived in Brooklyn when the children were very small. In Macon, we had a Volkswagen bus. I made a small table to replace the middle seat. It had a hinged top that folded over onto the back seat to make a bed. We all managed to sleep in the "bus" and traveled together to rustic campsites. We used a small hibachi grill when a campfire was impractical.

In those days our vacations were always the same. We traveled to Minnesota to see our families and enjoy the lake country. We usually stayed at a small resort on Rush Lake. From Brooklyn we traveled north to Niagara Falls, crossed into Canada and made good use of their beautiful free campsites. We crossed into Michigan and traveled across Wisconsin into Northern Minnesota.

Grandpa and Grandma Brattland lived in Wadena, Minnesota. Rush Lake was nearby so it was an easy trip for us to visit them. Grandma always gave each of the kids a dollar to go to the small neighborhood store to buy candy.

The lake had a small playground for the kids to enjoy and a small store to buy candy and supplies. We had our swimsuits, our canoe and our bicycles. That's all we needed. When Nancy was about 18 months old she wanted to do everything the boys did. They were going up and down the slide so she wanted in on the fun. She climbed to the top and fell off the side of the slide! I rushed under the slide to try to catch her and found her hanging on to a brace. She had strong hands and always loved to play on monkey bars.

Jon was a roamer. He roamed around the neighborhood in Denver and did the same at the Lake. A common question was, "Where's Jon?" I usually found him helping one of our camping neighbors carry their fishing gear or their fish in from the boat.

Matt loved to be in the water. He would play in the water for hours. He thought he was being tortured when he had to stay out of the water for an hour after lunch.

When we moved to Denver we continued to vacation at Rush Lake. As the kids grew, we had to take more gear with us. It was quite a sight to see our Toyota Corolla Wagon loaded with our canoe and four bicycles. One was on each side of the canoe on top of the car, one was in front and one was in back. Later, as the girls got older, we managed to add two more bicycles, one in front and one in back.

One year, we traveled to Yellowstone National Park and camped in our wagon. We had traded for a used Volkswagen to have space for our growing family. One morning we woke up, looked out into the woods, and were surprised to see a timber wolf staring at us. We were grateful for the safety of the vehicle.

One night we arrived at our campsite, set up our tent, and arranged our things. It was a beautiful evening and we had been traveling all day, so we decided to take a walk. We had purchased a watermelon as a treat to have with our supper. We made the mistake of leaving it on the picnic table. When we returned, a family of raccoons was sitting on our table enjoying our watermelon. We all agreed seeing them made it worthwhile. We threw the watermelon into the woods so they could enjoy it in peace.

We always traveled on a shoestring budget. One time, we took a trip to the Black Hills. Our last night on the road was rainy, so we camped near a shelter where we cooked our dinner. We filled our car with enough gas to get us home and had just enough money left to purchase some spaghetti noodles and sauce, but no hamburger. In our stash of food we had some bread and peanut butter and jelly to get us home the next day. Experiences like that are what make family memories great.

Bishop's Assistant

Macon was like a little bit of heaven on earth. But all good things come to an end—if there is to be a new beginning. The Bishop's assistant spoke to me a couple of time out of concern for me because I was in such a small church. He had great respect for what I had done there and said, "We would be happy to recommend you for any church in the Central District." I had found a comfort zone in Macon, and such suggestions seemed threatening. He wondered what it would take to change my mind.

The Central District Convention that year was held at the YMCA Center in Estes Park, Colorado. In a sense, it was like going home for me. I had run a back-packing program in the Rockies, and some of our trips originated at Estes Park. This Convention was held jointly by the ALC and the Lutheran Church in America (LCA) because we were working on a merger. We were integrated in every way possible, so my roommates were from the LCA. This was an important gathering because the District was electing a new bishop.

I always had a difficult time staying focused in the long convention sessions. This afternoon was no different, and I decided to take a hike to Bear Lake. It was a beautiful day. I couldn't resist getting out in the sunshine and mountain air. I was just returning from my delightful walk when one of my roommates came running to meet me. "They are calling your name to come to the stage," he said. He had wandered away from his LCA meeting too and overheard the call.

As I arrived at the convention hall, several men offered me their neckties. I learned that something very unlikely had happened. I had just been elected Vice President of the Central District. I knew before I left for my hike to Bear Lake that I had been nominated, but I thought there was very little chance that I would be elected. It didn't occur to me that I should be embarrassed about being caught skipping out on such an important part of the convention. The newly elected bishop was also on stage and we were introduced together.

After the applause had died down, and before he went to the mike to greet the convention, he leaned over and said to me, "Don't go anywhere…I want to talk to you about being one of my assistants."

That really surprised me. I waited around, and in due time we got together and I heard him say, "You and Bob are the two men I would really like to work with for the next six years."

Of course, I said the appropriate thing, "I'll pray about it and give it some serious thought." I called home to tell my wife what had happened. She was as surprised as I was.

When I got home, I told the children about the election and the offer of this new job. Their first question was, "Can we still live in Macon?" I said, "No, we would probably have to live in Denver or Lincoln or Omaha."

The boys were fine with the idea of the move, but the girls began to cry. They were worried about having to leave their friends. After giving it some time, I decided I would call the new Bishop and tell him we were just not ready to move.

He was persistent and said, "I'm not going to let you off the hook. I really want you to represent the Central District in Nebraska. We will establish a satellite office in Lincoln. It is very important. We will be completing the plans for the merger of our churches. You are the right person for this job."

Muriel and I spent lots of time talking about the pros and cons of moving, and we gradually decided that it was the right time for us. The children needed to get into a school and community with other people of color. My salary would triple at a time when our children were getting ready to enter college.

Unfortunately, we didn't own a home and we had no equity to bring for the purchase of a house. The Bishop and Bob had already thought that through. They knew a wealthy man in Lincoln who would be happy to loan us some money for a down payment. He did, and we finally agreed that I would accept the letter of call to be the Assistant to the Bishop.

The Bishop worked out an agreement with the congregation in Macon that would allow me to serve them half-time until school was out.

Muriel and I went to Lincoln to look for a house. We had set a maximum price we thought we could pay for our home, keeping in mind that we would start with a second mortgage. After riding around with a realtor for most of the day, we were discouraged. Everything we liked was far too expensive, and everything we saw in our price range was a dump.

The day was over. We were about to head for home without finding a house when the realtor stopped in front of a house with a "For Sale" sign. The lawn had not been taken care of for some time. Muriel said, "I like the looks of this house. Could we possibly see it?"

The realtor made a call and said, "Yes, I can show it to you, but I want you to know it lists as a two-bedroom home." We walked through the house and I could see in Muriel's eyes that she really liked it. It had been standing empty, and the realtor recommended that we limit our offer. Meanwhile my mind was working on how I could make this house work for our family. I could turn the attached single garage into a family room, convert the living room into a living room-dining room combination and turn the current dining room into a bedroom. The basement was unfinished but could, in due time, be finished with more bedrooms.

We put in a bid that was accepted. We learned it had been owned by an old couple who had entered a nursing home. Their kids were from out of town and were happy to accept our offer.

We were eager to show the house to our children. As soon as we got a key, we brought them to Lincoln for a camping trip in our new home. We brought air mattresses and sleeping bags and slept together on the living room floor. Pizza for supper was a natural.

I moved to Lincoln to live in the house and use my spare time to get it ready for the family. It needed some serious cleaning inside and out, and the decor was old fashioned. I re-papered a couple of the rooms and painted the dining room to look more like a bedroom.

Moving school children to a new city in June was difficult. The three who would still be at home missed their friends and spent a lot of time moping around the house with "nothing to do" (Matt was a counselor at Carol Joy Holling youth camp that summer). Muriel got them registered for school and then set out to explore Lincoln with them. Somehow they managed to get through the summer. We were amazed at how quickly they adapted once school started. It wasn't long before our house was full of friends, and we were happy to entertain them.

Muriel applied for a teaching job in Lincoln and some of the small towns nearby. No teaching positions were available, so she took a job as a para-professional working with severe and profoundly disabled children. She loved to work with these children and went back to school to get credentials to teach in that area. She soon had her own classroom, and the staff at Hawthorne Elementary School was great for her.

In the fall, Matt was off to Concordia College in Moorhead, Minnesota. He was the one who benefited most by the move from high school to college. He had no real friends in high school, but now he was thrilled to find roommates and other friends who had interests similar to his. What a treat it was for us to go to the annual Christmas concert at Concordia.

Jon went to Lincoln Southeast High School, just a couple of blocks from our house. Nancy went to Pound Junior High School and became involved with music and drama. Julie started at Rousseau Elementary School. They all found good friends.

138

Traveling in Five States

My work as an assistant to the Bishop was very different from anything I had done before. I had to sharpen up my knowledge of Robert's Rules of Order because, as the Vice President of the Central District, it was my job to chair meetings which usually included about 75 people, including representatives from five states.

One of my first tasks was to get a district car, since I would be driving about 60,000 miles a year around the five-state district. The District Treasurer called and told me to go pick out a car and then call him to arrange for the purchase. I picked out a used Ford and felt pretty good about the good buy I had found. He laughed at me and said, "No, that will not do!" Then he instructed me to go to the nearest Buick or Oldsmobile Dealership and purchase a NEW car, nothing smaller that a Buick LeSabre or an Oldsmobile Cutlass. I went to the Oldsmobile Dealer and found a beautiful new Cutlass that was champagne color with a cinnamon interior. After a short phone call the car was paid for and I was given the keys. It was a very strange feeling for me to drive away in style. I am a country boy not accustomed to such treatment.

Muriel thought it would be important for me to have a new suit. We went to the Men's Warehouse and got two suits for the price of one. I have never been a suit wearer, and I soon learned that I didn't need to wear those suits except in unusual circumstances. My customary blue jeans worked well in my new job.

I had an interesting dream some time in those first weeks on the job. In my dream, I was out on the prairie and could see what appeared to be a dust spiral spinning its way toward me. As it got closer I realized the dust was stirred up by a horse and carriage. As it came even closer, I realized it was a beautiful carriage with a steed decked out with lots of shiny chrome.

Suddenly, as the carriage stopped in front of me, the horse stumbled, broke loose from the carriage, and turned into a very large, fat pig. (It can only happen in a dream!) At that moment I did what you might expect a farm boy to do. I wrestled the pig this way and that and finally got it into a pen. When it was all over, I looked down at my dirty, torn clothes and realized I was dressed in one of my new suits.

I had studied some dream analysis and knew that a dream is related to the dreamer's life. It didn't take much analysis to understand where this dream came from. I was being pampered in so many ways in my new life and the dream expressed it all in a very humorous way. I tend to dream a lot, but that was one of the best and funniest dreams that I can remember.

My work on the Central District Staff centered in a satellite office in Lincoln. Nebraska had the most congregations in the five-state area we served. I was fortunate to share an office with Pearl Goldenstein, the coordinator of resources for the district. She and her husband, Erv, knew the history of the district and were a great resource for me. My job was to serve wherever the Bishop sent me. That meant I helped with the call process, assisted congregations in finding pastors, and met with congregations that were experiencing problems.

I developed a program that I called "Ministry Enrichment." In this program, the leadership of the congregation was asked to invite members to small group listening sessions. I brought with me a team of respected lay people from neighboring congregations. They joined me in the listening process on Fridays and Saturdays. On Saturday afternoon the listening team got together to compile a word picture of what we had been hearing. On Saturday evening we met with the church council and reported that "picture" to them. Then we met with the pastor and reported to him or her.

On Sunday morning I usually led worship and gave a report to the congregation. I made recommendations based on what we had heard. Sometimes this was a very delicate process, but I found that it worked well.

My family wasn't happy about how much time I had to spend away from home. They felt that if bad things were going to happen, they would happen when I was away. One sad event happened just before our move to Lincoln. Nancy's horse, Bucky, got sick and died in the pasture. We had a neighbor who was a horseman and knew exactly what to do. He called the vet to come out and assess what had happened. Then he called the rendering truck. Explaining to the children what was going to happen to Bucky's body was not easy.

Another time, I received a phone call at the congregation in Oklahoma where I was working. We didn't have cell phones in those days, so reaching me was never easy. I called back and found out that Nancy was in the hospital. She was very sick with mononucleosis. I raced across Oklahoma, Kansas and Nebraska to get home as soon as possible. I arrived in the middle of the night and was heartbroken to see how weak she was. I stayed home for a few days as she slowly recovered. Dads should never be gone when these things happen, but sometimes it can't be avoided.

On another trip, I was returning from Bird City, Kansas, one night and traveling across southern Nebraska, when my headlights revealed something in the middle of the road. It was a car that had flipped over on its top. I backed my car into the ditch so my lights would shine on the car for other drivers to see. Then I searched the area and found no one, so I assumed the driver had been taken to a nearby hospital. Fortunately, I was a runner. I left my car and ran two miles into town to the sheriff. We called a wrecker and got the car off the road with no further incident. The driver was a college student on his way home for the weekend. He had drifted off the road and his front bumper high-centered and flipped his car over. The sheriff was kind enough to let me use a phone to call my wife and explain why I was delayed.

Working with Bishop Wayne Weissenbuehler and Bob Berthelsen was a wonderful experience. They taught me things about the church that I could not have learned by myself. I will always be grateful to them.

Special blessings also came to me when I was privileged to work with leaders from other denominations. While I was the assistant to Bishop Wayne, I also worked closely with the Bishop of the Lutheran Church in America, Dennis Anderson. Together we collaborated with regional leaders of the Lutheran Church, Missouri Synod, the United Methodist Church, the Disciples of Christ (Christian Church) and the United Church of Christ.

I was often in a leadership role. Because my educational background and ministry experience were in community ministry, it was natural for me to respond to challenges through innovative projects. One memorable project was when we responded to the severe drought in neighboring states, South Dakota and Kansas. On one occasion, we coordinated a hay lift to feed starving cattle. Volunteer farmers went from farm to farm with their trucks to pick up donated hay. When their truck was full, they met other truckers and went together to deliver the hay as a gift to farmers in need. A common remark from our farmers was, "I'd much rather be on the giving end of this project than on the receiving end." I saw it as another version of, "It's better to give than to receive."

On another occasion, we delivered truckloads of corn. Farmers went from field to field challenging each other to donate corn during the harvesting process. Farmers drove their combines up to a truck and ran their auger for a certain number of seconds. It didn't take long to fill the volunteer trucks. Then the caravan of trucks headed for the famers in need and delivered the gift. I was amazed and pleased.

I hosted an ecumenical dinner at Dana College. After studying the rosters of denominations in Nebraska, I learned that many pastors had advanced degrees. I dreamed of creating a Rural Theological Education Network (called R-TEN for short). I invited the presidents of the seminaries that served our churches, the church leaders (Bishops or presidents), and all the people with advanced degrees. It was a wonderful evening. About ten percent of the invitees were women, all of whom were nuns from the Roman Catholic Church (most denominations did not have women pastors at that time.). The pastors and other leaders appreciated being recognized. I learned that most of them felt hidden and lonely in their small churches around the state. Technology had developed enough so that it was possible to teach from one location, such as the University of Nebraska, and connect with students in locations across the state. However, development of this program became overshadowed by the process of merging our Lutheran denominations, resulting in what we have now: The Evangelical Lutheran Church in America.

Now that those of us who were regional ministers have retired, we meet every few weeks to maintain the friendships we cherish.

Celebrating the Merger

The big event that happened in my tenure as assistant to the Bishop was the merger of the ALC, the Lutheran Church in America (LCA), and the Association of Evangelical Lutheran Churches (AELC). It was my task to represent the ALC in that process, so I worked directly with the Nebraska Bishop of the LCA. After being around me for a couple of weeks, he called Bishop Wayne and exclaimed, "You have saddled me with a loose cannon!" He had encountered the "irrepressible" me.

Bishop Wayne said to him, "Just be patient. Bud is really a good guy. I would have to say that Bud doesn't work <u>for</u> anybody, but you will discover what a privilege it is to work <u>with</u> him."

We were in the process of putting together plans for the Nebraska Assembly when we would approve the merger and elect a new Bishop for Nebraska. The LCA people had in mind an assembly that would meet at St. Paul United Methodist Church in Lincoln, which would seat about 1,500 people. I had in mind a venue that would seat 5,000 people. They had in mind an assembly that would celebrate our Lutheran heritage, with an emphasis on our past. I had in mind an assembly that would be forward looking, celebrating new opportunities for our future. The LCA bishop finally agreed to let me be in charge of planning an event at Pershing Auditorium in Lincoln.

To move from 1,500 to 5,000 would require several new "feeders," so I looked around for some great leaders to help me. My thought from the beginning was that we needed people of all ages to represent the whole church. We started by organizing a program to attract senior citizens. We had a dinner for seniors in the basement of Pershing Auditorium, which was well attended.

We wanted to have lots of forward-looking music. We found one of the best organists in the area and rented a portable organ. We organized a mass adult choir made up of singers from many churches. We asked the instrumental-music instructor from Midland College to lead an orchestra made up primarily of students. We asked the choral director from Dana College to direct a mass youth choir consisting of students from across the state. We had a children's march from several downtown churches through the streets to Pershing Auditorium. The police were kind enough to oversee our movement from the churches to Pershing. About 500 children were in the march. We asked the women of the church to bring hundreds of quilts to decorate the auditorium. We had an African choir from Swaziland that brought an international flavor to our gathering. It was a beautiful sight to see. It was especially fun to see the children and youth dressed in special t-shirts for the occasion. It was a memory maker.

Some years later, the Bishop had become the president of Trinity Seminary in Columbus, Ohio. He had the occasion to introduce me as a speaker at one of the seminaries. This time instead of calling me a "loose cannon," he introduced me as a "master pastor." That was very nice. Our relationship had come a long way.

Extending Our Family

During my time as pastor at Sheridan Lutheran, I became the chairman of the Board of Directors at Wartburg Seminary in Dubuque, Iowa. One night as we were finishing a session, the secretary slipped me a note that someone was waiting to see me. I went out in the hall and was surprised to find Iteffa Gobena.

Iteffa had been educated his entire young life in mission schools in Ethiopia. He was an outstanding student and was chosen to attend the mission seminary to become a native pastor in the Mekane Yesu Church. After he became a pastor, he was arrested along with many others and served time on a chain gang under the communist regime. When the tribes began to be successful in the civil war, all the pastors were released from prison.

After his released from prison, he was brought to this country for a couple of weeks for some R & R. He was placed in the Nebraska Synod, and I was appointed by the bishop as his host. During the time he spent with me, we became best friends. Now he was back, sent by the church in Ethiopia to work on a master's degree while the war raged back in his homeland. He and his wife, Almaz, had found a way to get their children out of the country, and he invited me to dinner at their apartment for a surprising conversation.

I met Almaz and the three children, Dawit, Wengel and Banti. After we had enjoyed a delicious Ethiopian feast, he asked me an important question. He explained about the war in their homeland. He told me about the fear they lived with that their children would die in the war, possibly being used as human shields. Then he asked, "Would you consider raising our children?"

I called Muriel to ask her opinion. She never hesitated. "Yes, of course we will!" So the children and their mother came to live with us. I wondered how they would do in school. It didn't take long for them to prove that I didn't have to worry. They came home with A's and learned English on the run – literally. In addition to being good students, the children were all great runners. I spent many happy hours watching them win races while in high school and later as athletes at the University of Nebraska.

Almaz finished her degree at Midland College and then went home to join her husband. The children have been a wonderful blessing for our family. Now, years later, Iteffa is retired, and we all consider ourselves just one big family.

When the process of organizing a new church was finished, the old districts no longer existed and my job as assistant to the bishop ended. During the last month of 1988, the interim pastor at Sheridan Lutheran Church, Lincoln, was having a very difficult time with about 100 confirmation students. He had never worked with that large a group and was trying to teach all of them in one setting all by himself. He called the Bishop and asked where he could get some help. Bishop Wayne asked me to go there to help organize a new confirmation program. What I didn't know at the time was that Bishop Wayne intended to give them my name as a candidate to become their senior pastor.

We re-organized the confirmation program, creating small groups led by parents. This was a pattern with long historical precedent, as Luther wrote his small catechism as an aid to parents who were responsible for teaching the basics of the faith to their children. The program worked well. Early in January I was interviewed by the call committee at Sheridan and became their senior pastor. It was a great relief for my wife and children to finally have me home with them.

Family in Columbus, Ohio

The move to Lincoln back in 1982 turned out to be the right move for us in several ways. Our family thrived in this new world. The schools offered more opportunities for the children. Nancy loved the drama and music programs in junior high. Julie found lots of new friends at the new elementary school, and we lived about a block away from Sheridan Lutheran Church so involvement in youth programs was easy.

It had been difficult for my three youngest children to leave Macon and move to Lincoln, but once school started, the transition became easier. It was a wonderful time in the life of our family as we soon began to celebrate one graduation after another. Nancy and Julie were both singers. They sang in vocal groups in high school and were chosen to attend summer music camp. To this day, one of the highlights of my life is to hear them sing.

Matt was away at Concordia College in Moorhead, Minnesota, and having the time of his life. After graduating he came home to Lincoln to spend a year with us before going off to Trinity Seminary in Columbus, Ohio. After a year of internship in Puerto Rico, he returned to Columbus to do doctoral studies at Ohio State University.

Nancy graduated from Lincoln Southeast High School and joined Matt in Columbus to attend Capital University. Two years later, Julie tried the University of Nebraska and then decided she would join Nancy at Capital.

Many of the "good times" in our family took place in Columbus. We spent some very memorable hours "doing" graduations and weddings. On each occasion we rented a set of motel rooms and moved to Ohio for a few days.

Matt attended Trinity Lutheran Seminary. He had an interest in studying theology and was a very good student. He studied Spanish and then went to spend a year as a student at a seminary in Argentina. He made some new friends there but had left one special friend behind in Ohio. He invited Monica to visit him in Argentina, and he proposed to her on a short cruise. Then they surprised everyone by secretly flying home and sharing their news in very creative ways with their families. They arranged with Julie to have us go for a walk in a park near our home and sit on a certain park bench with our eyes closed. When Julie told us we could open our eyes, Matt and Monica were there in front of us with the ring sparkling in the sun and love sparkling in their eyes. Muriel's moist eyes said it all. Romance will never go out of style.

Matt and Monica were married at the Seminary Worship Center in a beautiful ceremony with lots of wonderful music. We fell in love with Monica and her family, and we maintain family connections. One of the most interesting is Monica's mother and my sister, Ione. In a world where communication is easy, they correspond constantly.

Matt finished seminary and then went on to graduate school at The Ohio State University. When he received his Ph.D. I was honored to participate in the "hooding" ceremony.

Matt and Monica now make their home in Little Rock, Arkansas, and together they designed and built the most beautiful home I could ever imagine.

Nancy graduated from Capital University. She chose Columbus, Ohio, as a place to go to college because there was a significant population of Black people, more than just football players like Nebraska. But, she met and fell in love with a football player at Capital. When she married Charles, she married into a wonderful family. What a gift it was for us to meet Pat and Mom Beady. Nancy has a knack for making friends and building friendships that last. Many of them were involved, in one way or another, in their wedding. Pat and Mom Beady provided some delicious, but very spicy, hot wings for the groom's dinner. This was our first experience with hot wings. Nancy stayed at Capital University after graduation to work in the admissions office.

Julie also graduated from Capital University. Her field of interest was Criminal Justice. I'll never know how she got interested in Criminal Justice. She was my "little princess." I thought she should be a nurse or a pre-school teacher. Something safe. Later she gave me a card that said, "Thanks for teaching me that your 'little princess' can also be a slugger." She stayed in Columbus, so three of our four children made their home there for a time.

I have a favorite memory of Julie's days as a runner in junior high school. She had one competitor for the city championship in Lincoln in the quarter mile. She told me, "If I get my shoulder in front of her on the final turn, I can win." I watched with great interest as they ran down the back stretch. I wasn't surprised when Julie sprinted ahead of her competitor. It looked like she ran faster and faster as she came down to the finish line. I was proud when she won.

Julie was very interested in working out and staying in shape, so she spent some time at a workout center. She and Tate, the director of the center, developed a friendship, and soon they were engaged. They, too, had lots of friends at their wedding, and they were a beautiful couple. The friendship lasts but the marriage did not. I came back to Columbus, rented a truck, loaded Julie's possessions and moved her to Denver. There she studied to be a Veterinary Technician. She loved the work and fell in love with Denver. Unfortunately, she soon learned that Vet Techs don't earn much money. So, she transitioned back to Criminal Justice. I was proud, once again, when she finished her master's in Public Administration while working full time. Julie is always looking ahead to the next challenge.

The rest of the story is good news. She met the love of her life when she met Jason McKinney. It was New Year's Eve, and I was hosting an early supper at Granite City in Lincoln. I asked Jason to join us because his grandmother was in the hospital. Banti and Nicole were hosting a New Year's Eve party at their home and asked Julie and Jason to come. They started a conversation that just

155

wouldn't end. They both asked me, in different ways, "Could it be possible that we are already in love?" Time has proven that it is possible. They were married at a beautiful ceremony at Our Saviour's Lutheran Church in Lincoln.

A wonderful memory from that day was when guests were invited to release butterflies in honor of Muriel, and some of them landed on Julie's lovely wedding dress and in her hair.

Jon was the only one of our original four children who didn't move to Columbus. He stayed in Lincoln. He tried the University of Nebraska, but discovered he was not interested in college. He moved to St. Paul, Minnesota, to spend some time with his birth family, Frank and Deb Romero, and his three biological brothers, Randy, Roger and Robbie. He also spent some time with them in Arizona before moving back to Lincoln.

Jon likes physical labor and playing softball. I may be biased, but I think he is the best player in the over-50 league in Lincoln. He works with his friend, Mike, doing maintenance on Mike's rental apartments, mowing lawns in the summer, and removing snow in the winter. Jon and Renee were married on December 28, 2016.

Dawit graduated from Fremont High School and received an athletic scholarship to the University of Nebraska in Lincoln. Wengel graduated from Lincoln Southeast High School and then moved to Minneapolis to attend a community college. She went to work managing a store at the airport in Minneapolis. Banti graduated from Lincoln Southeast High School and joined his brother with an athletic scholarship at the University of Nebraska.

Dawit graduated with a degree in Mathematics and went to Denver to work. Wengel also moved to Colorado and lives near Dawit in Thornton. Banti graduated with a degree in Industrial Engineering and went to work for the Pella Corporation, headquartered in Shenandoah, Iowa. Today he works for TD Ameritrade in a management position.

All three of the kids from Ethiopia married, and each of them has two children—beautiful, intelligent grandchildren for us to share!

Ministry at Sheridan

When we moved to Lincoln, we bought a house about two blocks from Sheridan Lutheran Church, so it was logical for us to become members at that time. When I was later called to be their pastor, my family was more familiar with the congregation than I was.

The congregation had completed a remodeling project that included a large great hall between the sanctuary and the fellowship hall. I was excited because it looked like a great place to welcome the public into our space. I soon realized that not everyone felt the same way. Except for my years in Macon, I was a core-city pastor since starting my ministry in Brooklyn. The neighborhood around the church in Lincoln was changing rapidly. When the church was started, it was located on the south edge of Lincoln. It was in the country club area surrounded by beautiful homes. Now some of those homes were being sub-divided into apartments.

The original members of Sheridan had a vision of what their church should become. They felt that a church of about 500 people was big enough and at that point the congregation should start a new mission church. That is what they did, and they started Southwood Lutheran Church on South 27th Street. But Sheridan continued to grow, and that became a source of tension. At the same time, a group of church members dreamed of moving further east into a rapidly growing area of Lincoln.

I felt we should stay where we were on Sheridan Boulevard and minister to the changing neighborhood. I had my assistants take training, as I had done, to become members of the Police Chaplaincy. I learned later that quite a few people were unhappy when they saw the police chaplaincy car in our church parking lot. They thought the time spent doing chaplaincy work detracted from our ministry to members.

Another concern of some of our members was how we were sharing our building with the neighborhood. The Great Hall was a perfect place to enroll children in a neighborhood soccer program. Families could come in one door and go out the other, so traffic flow was not a problem. Mud was a problem, however.

We hosted many neighborhood organizations like Cub Scouts, Boy Scouts, Girl Scouts, and Brownie Scouts. Some members objected because "children are very hard on a church building." That became a serious issue when we were approached about the use of our building for a childcare center. A lady had been running the program in another building until it was condemned by the fire department. She needed a new space, but she also wanted to sell her childcare program. I put together a plan for us to buy it and change its name to the Sheridan Child Development Center. Opposition came from two directions: those who felt we should protect our building, and those who felt our kitchen was inadequate to serve the needs of the children. I learned that the small kitchen was intentional because "a church kitchen was never intended as a place to prepare food." My solution was to remodel the kitchen so it could be a place to prepare food.

Another issue that caused some problems was the need for sponsors to assist refugee families. The congregation council never supported the sponsorship of refugees, although a small task force of members took up the cause. Muriel and I used our home as temporary housing for several refugees as we helped them settle in Lincoln. This ministry was a great blessing to us and to the others who were involved. These refugees remain a blessing to me until this day.

The first two refugees to come to our home were Adis Behmen and Haris Tanovic. I remember the first breakfast I prepared for them. I wanted it to be special, so I made eggs, bacon, pancakes, coffee, and juice. They asked if I had any bread and cheese. They were looking for a simple breakfast that included strong coffee, French or Italian bread, and a chunk of cheese. Eventually, Adis moved to Las Vegas, Nevada, and raised his family there. Haris earned his engineering degree from the University of Nebraska and went to work for the Caterpillar Corporation. His work has taken him to Europe and back to America. He lives with his wife Katie and three children in Illinois.

Haris told me about his sister, Amila. He asked if we might be willing to sponsor Amila and Samir and their baby, Hana. I'll never forget how excited Haris was when we went to the airport to pick them up. He purchased a stuffed animal for Hana. When they came off the plane, they were obviously exhausted, but they fit into our family perfectly.

Samir and Amila were industrious from the start, and Samir went right to work delivering pizza and working at the Tool House doing menial tasks. When his boss at the Tool House discovered Samir was a good graphic designer, he started having him design covers for the annual catalogue. He entered one of the covers in a Corel's World Design Contest and The Best of The Year in Corporate ID Category. He has done very well in the corporate world. Amila has a degree in economics and has worked many years as Finance Director for Friendship Home, a shelter for abused women and children. What a joy it was to be with them when the twins, Ema and Naila were born. They are now students at the University of Nebraska, Lincoln.

Then we sponsored Majda Obradovic and her two daughters, Lana and Lea. Lana spoke several languages fluently at age 16.

162

Both girls did very well in college and Lana went on to teach at the University in Seoul, South Korea. Lea went to Germany where she produces documentary films. I am thrilled to have Lana back in Nebraska. She teaches at the University of Nebraska, Omaha.

We are all one family. I am as proud of all of them as I am of my own children.

Yet another point of contention within the congregation arose out of my work as a police chaplain. I had many contacts with Friendship Home, a ministry to women and children who had suffered abuse. One woman came to Lincoln with three daughters who were approaching their teens. She needed a four-bedroom home because the housing authorities determined that each of them needed their own bedroom. The financial assistance that was offered did not provide enough money to rent a four-bedroom apartment, so she and her girls came to live with us.

A small task force of members stepped up to solve the problem. We formed the Sheridan Housing Corporation, raised a little money, and purchased a house. Then we remodeled it to provide adequate space for this family of four. It served its purpose well, and this mother was able to complete her education and eventually become a teacher in the Lincoln Public School System.

Our children brought friends home who were facing various difficulties in their lives. We made room for several. This was not new to us because we had done the same thing in Denver and in Macon. Nancy brought her best friend, Julie Novak, home and asked if she could stay with us until she graduated from Southeast High School. "Please, Dad, she can share my room!" She did, and she was a delightful addition to our household. Now we had two Julies.

One of the best things that happened to me while I was at Sheridan was meeting Ben and Kathy Paisley. Kathy made our dreams for a quality children's program at Sheridan Lutheran Church come true, and Ben made one of my childhood dreams come true.

As a child I was pre-occupied with the fact that I was so small for my age. Whenever I ran across a "Charles Atlas" ad in a comic book, I dreamed of growing big and weighing 190 pounds so no one could ever "kick sand in my face again."

Ben invited me to see his workout room and began to teach me how to lift weights without hurting myself. I had a workout bench tucked away in my garage. I set up my workout space and began to put to work what he had taught me. I weighed about 150 pounds. Before long I weighed 155...then 160...then 165...then 170.... About that time my doctor noticed that I was gaining weight and wondered why. I told him it was all intentional. He cautioned me to remember that putting on weight, even if it is solid muscle weight, puts extra stress on my heart.

I was having too much fun to slow down! I weighed 175...then 180...then 185...then 190. I think I weighed about 192 when I had a heart attack, followed immediately by five by-passes. The doctor was right, but no one will ever be able to take away the fun of lifting weights…with results! It gave new meaning to what it was to have a "six pack."

Later, a friend told me he was talking to a new young pastor about the prison ministry that Pastor Bud had started. The pastor asked, "Who's Pastor Bud?" Before my friend could answer, he said, "Oh, I know, he's the one with the big shoulders!" (How cool was that!)

Ben gave me another gift as well. As a farm boy I could not participate in high-school athletics because we lived too far from school and there was always work to do at home. One day Ben asked if I was interested in playing basketball. A group of men played basketball at the Lincoln Lutheran High School gym. I was already in my sixties, but the invitation was too good to ignore. I really enjoyed playing with these "younger" men and held my own fairly well. I learned a lot from playing basketball, including the importance of watching for elbows. One night I went for a rebound and a very tall, talented player caught me above the eye. The blow knocked me out. When I came to, the other players were busy looking for towels and ice. They took me to the hospital, and a young doctor demonstrated his stitching skill on my eye. The humorous ending to the story was that I had a very important funeral the next morning. My dear friend, Erv Goldenstein, had died. He was well known in Lincoln and there was a very large crowd, as expected. I had a black eye that extended down my neck and shoulder into my chest. I wore dark glasses, but there was no way to hide the shiner.

As time went on, there was growing criticism of my leadership at Sheridan. Each president brought a new issue to the table. I eventually realized that the biggest issue was the desire of a growing number of members to move the church to a new, growing neighborhood.

One president was critical of my preaching. She asked me if I had ever taken a preaching course. She asked, "Would you be open to taking a speech course at the University?" It was just a coincidence that at that same time, a preaching seminar was underway at Dana College. The professor asked the class if there was someone they would like to invite to preach at the celebration at the end of the course. They suggested me! I went there to preach and received an enthusiastic response. I never told them about my critics back home.

The Nebraska Synod Bishop, Richard Jessen, was kind enough to stay in touch with me through some of these difficult times. He was very supportive while he dealt with the leaders at Sheridan. One day he came to visit me and informed me about his visit to the prison congregation at the State Prison in Sioux Falls, South Dakota. He said, "I was really impressed with what I saw happening there and came back to share my experience with the Synod Council. They agreed, and quickly added, 'We know the perfect pastor to start a prison ministry here in Lincoln.'" They were talking about me.

At that same time, I was having discussions with the Sheridan Executive Committee. I told them, "I think your problem will be solved soon. The Bishop is working on an idea with the Synod

Council that involves me and my future. I'm not free to share anything about it until it is official and the Nebraska Synod Council is ready to issue a call." As it turned out, it didn't take long before I started training for work at the Nebraska State Penitentiary.

That set Sheridan free to call a pastor who would help them move to a new neighborhood and build a new church. They sold the old building to the Roman Catholic Church, found just the right pastor, and launched a new building project. Visit the new Sheridan Lutheran Church and you will know that the results were magnificent.

Horseshoe Lake

It was never our intention to live on a lake. On a Sunday afternoon in June 1997, we were scheduled to visit a farm. Our hope was to find a five-acre farm site where we could build a small home, raise a garden, and have a few animals. I thought a horse would be nice, and a couple of llamas.

While we were waiting, Muriel was paging through the ads in the newspaper. She found a lake cabin. She said with a smile, "It must be a dump, because it is in our price range." We decided to check it out. We called the realtor and he said, "If you hurry, I'll wait here for you." When we arrived at the cabin, we experienced this wonderful serenity. We both noticed it. As the realtor showed us the cabin, I knew Muriel had fallen in love with it.

We saw a two-bedroom cabin with one large living room and a small office. The living area included a kitchen with a small island. An old boathouse stood at the end of the cabin. It had not been used for years, and the doors at both ends barely hung on. The lake lot was quite large, so there was room for a garden.

As Muriel explored every inch of the cabin, my mind was working on how we could make this our home. I saw potential for a dining room-sitting room combination in the boathouse. On the

168

beach sat an old fishing boat with the transom rotted away and a paddle boat. I knew my canoe would fit perfectly. My mind pictured a garage with a carport on either side and storage space upstairs. We could build it in the garden space.

Muriel had always wanted to have a cabin on a lake. She looked at me with pleading eyes and said, "What do you think?" I said, "I have some ideas that could make it work." The realtor explained that the lower-than-expected price was because the cabin was on a leased lot. We would own the building but not the land. In very little time we made up our minds. We didn't want to haggle over the price and risk losing this opportunity, so we offered exactly what was asked. The deal was done.

We weren't aware when we made the offer that loan companies did not give home loans for houses on leased land. Our realtor explained that the local bank would give us a loan at a higher interest rate. We decided we could live with that.

We moved into our new home, and Muriel loved it as much as she thought she would. The serenity came with the cabin at no extra cost. I went right to work designing the garage and carports. As it turned out, I never used it as a garage. It became my shop. When we were in the process of building it, I was working on the roof when I noticed the sun going down in the west. It occurred to me that with a few adjustments I could arrange a nice guest room in the upstairs space. I put a double door upstairs on the west end of the shop and added a deck. We had enough storage upstairs on each wing to suit our needs. If you sit on the deck, you are looking west, down the length of the lake, toward the sunset. The sunsets are amazing.

Later I made good on a promise to convert the boat house to a dining room-sitting room combination. Our cabin had become a very comfortable home.

Muriel and I always loved water. Every day we found time to paddle our canoe around the lake. Our children found time in their busy schedules to come home to visit and bring the grandchildren. As we remodeled, Charlie, our grandson, was concerned. He asked, "Is it still going to be a cabin?" The word "cabin" held a special appeal to him and to us.

Now, many years later, we have guests come to visit us from time to time. Many people comment on how peaceful it is. It is a little hard to know where that peacefulness comes from. We have a busy railroad on the south side of our home—with loud whistles. We have Interstate 80 on the west with the constant sounds of commerce. Nature, however, seems to have a way of overwhelming those distractions.

On a typical morning I get up early and step outside. I usually stop for a few moments to take in the still beauty of the morning before putting on my life jacket. I wonder what nature has in store for me today. I pick up my canoe paddle and a small weight for the front of the canoe and head down to the beach. My first thought is, "Lord, here we are again." I know where the serenity comes from. It is a gift from above, and my canoe is a great place to meditate.

I'm always aware that I'm not alone. Deer may be watching me from the trees. I know somewhere along the shore there are several fishermen, none of them human. If I watch carefully, I will see a great blue heron and some smaller little green herons. Because I disturb the natural scene with my presence, I'll hear the chatter of a kingfisher looking for breakfast. Dozens of birds wake up with the dawn. Robins are the most noticeable, but the sounds of blue jays, cardinals, chickadees, nuthatches, grackles, finches, orioles, and kingbirds soon fill the air. On rare occasions a bald eagle will soar high overhead, looking down with an eagle eye for breakfast. Cormorants, fish-eating ducks, roost in the cottonwood trees. We are very fortunate to have a pair of wood ducks nesting in the trees above our home.

If I'm lucky, I will see the beaver who makes his home in the swampy area near the lake. A muskrat family lives in a hole under a tree across the lake. I can hear the wild turkeys in the woods nearby, talking softly as they forage for food. If I sit very still, I can hear the wolves in the Prairie Safari on the hill as they eat their morning rations.

Usually, the Canada geese honor me with a few flyovers while I enjoy my canoe ride. Each year we have about four families of baby geese on the lake. It is fun to watch mom and dad bring their babies down to the water for the first time. Their little legs can't carry them as fast as they seem to want to go, and so they tumble into the water. But as soon as they get to the lake, they are right at home. "Look Mom, I can swim!" The families number from one to ten little ones. It is a joy to watch them grow. The babies appear about the first of April and they are ready to fly in mid-July. At first they fly over in family groups. Later they fly in larger groups and learn to fly in formation.

When my canoe ride is over, I return to the cabin. Ruth has coffee ready and we share our morning breakfast. Now that I'm retired, I have plenty of time to return to the lake for a ride on the pontoon. Mine is a mini-pontoon, six by eight feet, with two seats. I can squeeze two lawn chairs on the front, if necessary.

The beach at our cabin is three-tiered. The lowest level is the beach itself, where the boats are stored. The second level is a sandy area where children can play with beach toys without being near the water. The third level is our lawn where old people like me can sit and enjoy the scene without getting too close to the action.

A Canoe Ride on Horseshoe Lake

Every evening I check the weather report to see what I can expect for my morning canoe ride. Three conditions keep me from going out on the lake: hail, wind and lightning. I live with two seasons: the season of hard water (ice) and the season of soft water. Fortunately, I can start canoeing around the first of March and continue until the middle of December. The season of hard water lasts, in an average year, about three months.

Horseshoe Lake is in a valley. That allows most of the wind to pass over us. I can see the flag at Mahoney State Park from the lake. The flag is rarely still in the morning, but the lake is usually quiet before the sun comes up.

I set out my canoe clothing the night before. In the fall, that means long underwear, blue jeans, lined flannel shirt, lined jacket, stocking cap, lined leather gloves, and a life jacket. When I step outside, I pause to take in the beauty of the morning.

Each morning is beautiful in its own way. For example, as I write this, the last two days had me canoeing in a soft gentle rain one day and enjoying a clear sky with a clear view of Pegasus, Orion, the Southern Cross, the Big Dipper, Cassiopeia, a full moon, and a couple of planets the next.

Each morning I pick up my beautiful ergonomic canoe paddle, (thanks to Matt and Monica, my son and daughter-in-law), and a twenty-five-pound dumbbell. The dumbbell goes in the front of the canoe to keep the bow in the water. It helps keep the canoe on course. My pacemaker demands that I move slowly. One morning I bent down to put the dumbbell in the canoe and stood up too fast. I momentarily lost my balance and fell backward into the lake. The water was still cool, not cold, and I climbed back on the beach and went inside to change into dry clothes. For years my children had encouraged me to wear a life jacket when I went on the water. I finally got the message.

It is a magic moment each morning when I push off from the beach. I marvel at the majesty of creation. I pause to say thank you to the Creator and say my morning prayer.

Lord, I want to be your man today.
I want to give honor and glory to you by what I do and say,
I want to bless people along the way.
I want what I do today to have good consequences for tomorrow:
I want to grow,
I want to learn,
I want to build,
I want to become the man you created and redeemed me to be.

Rarely do we have any mosquitoes, even on a hot, humid morning, because there are few spots along the lake where water stands for mosquitoes to hatch. I'm sure the swallows help a great deal. There are thousands of swallows nesting under the interstate bridge across the Platte River. I read somewhere that swallows eat three times their weight in bugs every day.

My canoe is about sixty years old but is as good as new from my perspective. It glides easily along the quiet surface of the lake. After all these years of practice, I'm an expert at paddling. Together we are a perfect match. I paddle around to the far side of the horseshoe, trying not to disturb the geese and any other creatures that make their home on the lake. Grebes and cormorants entertain me as they dive for food. As I bend around the middle of the horseshoe, I keep my eyes on the shoreline, hoping to see the muskrat. Then I follow the shoreline to the far end of the lake and back to our beach. The canoe glides easily up onto the beach. The paddle becomes a temporary cane to steady me as I step carefully out of the canoe. I thank God for another new day. I tip the canoe over and turn it so it is ready for the next ride. Then I put my paddle, life jacket and dumbbell away for another day.

Followers of Christ Church

I left Sheridan to start a prison congregation at the Nebraska State Penitentiary. I attended the staff training course with a new group of trainees. The criminal justice system didn't really know what to do with me because I wasn't a state employee. My letter of call and my salary came from the Nebraska Synod Council. The Bishop had negotiated the plan with the Director of Corrections to start a prison congregation, but information didn't reach the warden or the coordinator of religious life (chaplain) at the penitentiary. When I first arrived, I was given an appropriate set of keys and a radio like all other employees. Soon the chaplain complained that if I had these privileges, all other volunteers would want them too. So, even though I was a full-time worker, my keys and my radio were taken away, and I was totally dependent on the chaplain. If it was his day off, I was not allowed into the prison. If I wanted to go to visit a prisoner, I had to ask his permission.

I received permission to start a prison congregation, but the prison called it a "class" like so many other classes. My congregation grew, and one Saturday night we had a naming session. The prisoners suggested lots of potential names until one prisoner said, "This is a difficult place to be a follower of Christ.

Why don't we call ourselves 'Followers of Christ.'" There was a boisterous round of applause, and that became their unanimous choice for our new name.

It took some time for me to win the trust of the institution, but it took very little time to win the trust of the inmates. Prisoners would pass the word about my presence, and an increasing number of them sent "kites", or a written request, asking to come to the chapel to see me. Others who were in lock-down units sent kites asking me to come to visit them in their cells. It was difficult for me to move around the institution because I had no keys and no radio. For example, if the chaplain wouldn't help me by calling the unit to tell them I was coming, I had no radio to ask them to open the gate for me. Instead, I walked toward the unit to find a staff member in the yard who would call for me. Some were friendly and happy to help. Others said things like, "Look, we don't owe you anything," and refused to help. Then I sent a kite to the prisoner and apologized for not making the visit.

Gradually, unit managers became accustomed to me being around and welcomed my visits. One manager said, "I like it when you come. The lights seem brighter when you are here, and the men are on their best behavior."

It was a common practice, when a prisoner "lost it" for some reason, to place him in a padded cell until he settled down. One day I received a call at the chapel asking if I would come to a unit where a prisoner was angry and threatening staff members. The chaplain wondered why they wanted me but let me respond. When I got to the unit, the manager said, "He asked to see you.

What we're going to do is let you meet with him in the commons area. We will be watching the whole time to make sure you are safe." I said, "I'm happy to visit with him, but would you mind taking the cuffs off of him?"

We visited for nearly an hour and, as we talked, he became calm. Finally, the unit manager said, "I'm sorry, Pastor Bud, but we have to stop now. It's about time to serve supper."

As the prisoner got up to leave, he gave me a big hug and asked if he could see me again tomorrow. Then, as he went back to his cell, he apologized to everyone he met for making threats and causing a disturbance. That event seemed to be a turning point in my relationship with the prison.

Bridges to Hope

One of the issues related to my ministry with prisoners had to do with the work I started on the outside of the prison. Every week prisoners were dismissed with nothing more than $100 gate pay. If they didn't have anyone on the outside to meet them and help them get a new start, they were in immediate trouble. They needed clothing, shoes, a place to stay, food to eat, transportation to apply for work, and help to get their driver's license. It was a joke to some of the workers who said to prisoners as they left, "We'll leave the light on for you." That seemed cruel to me, but it was based on fact. Most of them returned to prison in a very short time.

Muriel and I, with the support of our Nebraska Synod friends, decided to try and help a few of them. As I traveled around to churches in Nebraska, we received donations for the program we first called "The Bridge."

We gathered furniture, clothing, and household items and stored them in the shed in our back yard. Volunteers came to help us, and Stephens and Smith Construction Company gave us a storage unit. Soon we needed another storage unit, and they donated that one also. As the program grew, we soon needed to rent a warehouse so things were more accessible.

The chaplain at the prison knew we were breaking a rule for volunteers. Technically, we were not allowed to work with prisoners both inside and outside the prison. However, we had made an agreement with the Director of the Department of Corrections to work on the outside. That message didn't get to the chaplains, so I was warned that my work at the prison would soon come to an end. I tried my best to explain what we were doing and why, but they weren't buying it. One day I got an invitation (more like an order) to meet with the chaplains of all corrections institutions in Nebraska. That surprised me because I had never met with them before. I knew something was wrong so I was worried about how this would go. They didn't waste any time in getting to the point. They had decided that my work at the prison was over. They explained the rules to me, and to them, it all made good sense.

Just prior to this meeting, I had met with the Director of the Department of Corrections and had received a $15,000 grant to do work outside the prison. I think you can imagine the look on the faces of the men around the table that morning when I shared that news with them. They excused me and went on with their other business.

I had not registered the name, "The Bridge," so it wasn't long until some other group chose that same name. The board changed our name to "Bridges to Hope."

In those early days we received some financial support from congregations and individuals, but most of the support came from Muriel and me.

Muriel was an outstanding teacher. One year, she even received an award as the outstanding Special Education Teacher in Lincoln.

Muriel retired from teaching in 2000 but decided to go back to teaching and donate her salary to support The Bridge. That worked well for a couple of years, and we, with the help of some wonderful volunteers, helped a lot of men. (In the early days of the program we worked only with men because I worked at the Nebraska State Penitentiary.)

Some of the volunteers bought a house, and we made an attempt at providing some temporary housing. Later we added another house and two rented apartments. That did not work well. It took too much time and energy for me to supervise. I naively thought I could rely on the men to supervise themselves as they started new jobs. The lure of drugs and alcohol was much too strong, and we had far too many encounters with the police. I was called into town nearly every night to deal with tenant problems.

Bridges to Hope has continued to grow under the leadership of the Board of Directors and the help of many volunteers. Now we have a large warehouse in south Lincoln. Rhonda is the

Executive Director, and Kathy is the office manager. The two of them have created a new store called *Bud's Thrift Shoppe*. For many years we collected donations of all kinds from the public. If something didn't fit our needs, we gave it away to other thrift stores. Now we have a thrift store of our own where we can sell to the general public. The income from the store goes to support Bridges to Hope.

The Unthinkable

An unthinkable problem developed in the late summer of 2002. I was called to Culler Middle School because Muriel was not feeling well, and I took her to the doctor. He said, "This doesn't look good. We will need to do exploratory surgery." They took her to surgery and discovered that she was filled with cancer. The doctor explained that she had mesothelioma and that it would take her life, possibly before the end of the year. She said to the doctor, "Are we going to just let it happen and do nothing?" The doctor explained that there was no treatment for this type of cancer, although a treatment was being tested. The doctor explained, "It will be very expensive because it will not be covered by insurance."

I knew we had to try. It was part of Muriel's nature to fight any enemy, including incurable cancer. We soon learned that the treatment was not only doing no good, it was making her sicker. The children came home for Thanksgiving and we had a nice dinner at home. They came again for Christmas, but by this time Muriel was not able to sit at the table with us.

I know that she had an idea much earlier that something was not right. She had made a list of things she valued, and she

186

identified which of the children should receive each item when she was gone. She also wrote a thank you letter to the children, and now she asked me to give it to them. Here is a copy of her letter:

Dear Children,

I want to write to you at this time to be sure you know how much I love you. You have been such an important part of the joy in my life. How I loved to watch you grow, and now you have become all grown up and are loving and caring people.

I also want you to know that I'm not afraid of dying. I know that Jesus has provided me with his purity by dying on the cross, and because of that kind of love I will see God, and go to spend eternity with him. I want each of you to believe in that also, and know that God has forgiven you for no matter what, and loves you beyond any love we may have experienced.

I want you to walk in his love and give this love to all those around you.

I thank you for my beautiful grandchildren, and I see how you love and care for them. I know they will grow up to be strong, loving people because of your care. God give you strength and peace as you continue to raise them.

May God bless you and be near you in all you do.

I love you,

Mom

I contacted a local hospice organization for some help and decided I would take care of my dear wife as long as I could. My sister came to stay with me. I rented a hospital bed and situated it in the living room so Muriel could see out the window. One very strange thing happened. She loved to see cardinals, and they often visited our bird feeder. A pair of cardinals came every day and hopped around on our deck. It was almost like they were there to visit her. When she was gone, they never came back. One year later, on the anniversary of her death, they were back for a one-day visit. They haven't been back to our deck since.

Muriel died early in the morning on February 7, 2003. I had placed my recliner next to her bed so I could be there to watch over her. During that night, I had a troubling dream that Muriel was crawling across a meadow toward a bridge. I wanted to go with her and help her, but I couldn't. She crawled up on the bridge and someone came from the other side. I knew it was our Lord Jesus. He met her, took her by the hand, and they stood up and walked together. Then she started to skip like a child.

I was not happy. In fact, I was momentarily angry with God. That is what I wanted to do! I wanted to take her by the hand and see her walk again. I wanted to skip like a child with her. But instead I was surrounded by a quiet emptiness that is hard to define. It wasn't just sadness.

I woke from the dream and touched her arm. It was cold. I woke my sister and my son to tell them. I called the hospice office, and they came to help take care of contacting the authorities.

The quiet emptiness of my dream stayed with me for a long while. Over time, though, the emptiness has been slowly replaced with memories, with thanksgiving for our children and grandchildren, with appreciation for a life well lived and shared, with music that continues to bless people, and with a sense that all people are our brothers and sisters and that the love of God encompasses us all.

One of the things the prisoners missed was the music she brought to the prison worship on Saturday evenings. She wore her Sunday best and sang songs that brought 100 prisoners to a hush. She sang songs that were classics in the church: *Amazing Grace, Ave Maria, The Lord's Prayer, Jerusalem, I Know That My Redeemer Liveth,* and *O Holy Night.* It was my honor and privilege to accompany her on the piano.

When we were struggling during some difficult times in our lives, she gave to me a poster that said, "One Rose Can Be My Garden." She loved the saying, "Bloom where you are planted." She also said, "Sometimes the best thing that can happen to us is to find ourselves 'planted' in a manure pile, rich with nutrients for future growth!" She said, "When the going gets tough, you trudge." She meant you don't sit down in the mud and pout; you keep trudging because better days are always ahead.

The world is a better place because of the gifts she shared.

We had many wonderful friends in our lifetime together. Two of the very best were Jim and Arlene Grosch. They were very helpful to us, especially with hosting refugees. They were both intelligent, and creative. Arlene wrote wonderful poetry. She wrote this poem for Muriel.

For Muriel

What do those eyes see now;
Those eyes that crinkled at a child's play
And softened at its pain
That leapt with mischief or a dare
And laughed at gentle jibes?
What do those eyes see now;
Those soldier's eyes, the steady gaze
That spoke of trudging on
That lent protection to the frail
And courage to the faint?
What do those eyes see now;
Those eyes so fierce at unjust ploy

That fought against the tide
That clearly saw a person's heart
And found no gift in blame?
What do those eyes see now?
Those curious eyes that sought to know
That wanted to know why and how
That fit with wonder at the earth
And glowed at far-flung stars?
What do those eyes see now?

II Corinthians 13:12: For now we see through a glass darkly but
then face to face.

Arlene

The FEAST

Another special ministry that joined Followers of Christ Church (at the penitentiary) and Bridges to Hope was the FEAST.

The FEAST is a program at my home congregation, Our Saviour's Lutheran Church in Lincoln. It grew out of my loneliness. Muriel was gone. I looked around for things to do. I thought long and hard about my personal prayer: Lord, I want to be your man today.

I want to give honor and glory to you with what I do and say.

I want to bless people along the way...

It was difficult to get myself up on Sunday morning to go to church alone. I decided to pick up some of my friends from the Lincoln Community Correction Center. I had a Dodge Caravan that could carry six passengers comfortably, and seven if they squeezed together in the middle seat. My plan was to take them to church with me and take them out to dinner at Village Inn. The management gave me a large corner table so we could have time and space together on Sunday afternoon. I could teach Bible study, or we could talk about plans for the future.

My plan worked well for a couple of weeks. On the third Sunday, the Pastor stopped me to ask what I was doing. He made it clear that people knew these men must be prisoners since they were coming to church with me. I explained my plan. He asked if I would mind coming to the congregation council meeting. I wondered if I was in trouble. I wondered if people were upset about the prisoners coming to church.

I went to the council meeting to explain my plan. They said something like this: "You don't have to take them to Village Inn. We would gladly supply the dinner." One of the council members was a wonderful cook. He and his wife invited me and the prisoners to their house. I still remember the menu. We enjoyed pork roast injected with flavors like apricot. The meal ended with homemade pie. That was much better than Village Inn.

The next Sunday someone else did the cooking and we ate at the church. Meanwhile, the congregation council was forming a plan. They hired a man to coordinate the dinners and they recruited people to become sponsors. They didn't need me to provide meals, and they didn't need me to provide transportation. In a very short time, the congregation bought a used bus. They sent members out to the Community Correction Center for orientation to become sponsors. They picked up an increasing number of prisoners, whom they re-named "partners." With the partners, they decided on a name for the program: The FEAST. FEAST stands for Friends Eating and Studying Together. That soon became Friends Eating and Studying, Singing, and Serving Together.

I am amazed that volunteers have maintained the FEAST program all these years. Other congregations have stepped up to help provide meals. On a typical Sunday noon, they serve dinner to over one hundred partners and members of their families.

After dinner, they have a community meeting in which they share a sing-along and celebrate birthdays, anniversaries, families being reunited, partners getting parole, partners finding work, and partners finding apartments. After a time of prayer, they go to classes. When the allotted four hours are over, the bus takes them back to the Center.

We made some mistakes along the way. For example, we once served poppy seed dressing on the salad. Afterward, the partners didn't pass the drug test to get back into the Correction Center. It was our fault and we took the blame. However, the partners were told they should know better than to eat poppy seed dressing.

The members of Our Saviour's Lutheran Church treat the prisoners like equals. If you go there to worship, you probably won't know that the reader is a prisoner or that the greeters are prisoners. It's a beautiful ministry.

This ministry didn't come without cost. A few people left the congregation because of the prisoners. The council, however, felt that was a small price to pay for a dynamic outreach ministry.

Freed for LIFE

To support prison ministry, Muriel had gone back to teaching to donate her salary. When she was no longer around to provide financial support, I wanted to do something in her memory to keep the programs going.

I started a fund-raising program which I named Freed for LIFE, with the proceeds going toward "Muriel's Fund." I hosted a dinner at the Lancaster Event Center and invited people from the churches to attend. I set very large goals, hoping in time to raise a million dollars for Muriel's Fund. In those days the interest rates were high, and I thought it would be practical to use the annual interest to keep the programs going.

We all know what happened to the interest rates. Later I was forced to use the principal in Muriel's Fund to keep Bridges to Hope alive.

We continue to host a Freed for LIFE dinner on the second weekend in November. Through the years the men's group at Sheridan Lutheran Church has provided the meal. Good people continue to come from miles away to stay in touch and bring their donations. I am so very thankful for their support.

In 2018, we were very fortunate to have Shon Hopwood as our speaker. Shon grew up in David City, Nebraska, and became a bank robber. He went to federal prison and while there became interested in the law library. After a few years of reading law books, he realized he had not only an interest in law, but a knack for writing legal briefs to help fellow prisoners. One of his cases went to the Supreme Court. He was successful and the Court was very impressed with his work. To make a long story short, he got out of prison, became a lawyer and now teaches at the Law School at Georgetown University. Because of him, many new people became excited about our dinner this fall.

Freed for LIFE, Bridges to Hope, the FEAST, Followers of Christ Church, and Bud's Thrift Shoppe all work together toward the common goal of supporting men and women as they prepare to leave prison and walking with them as they start their new lives.

Rhonda and Kathy do an amazing job, working with the Board of Directors to keep the ministry going. Many volunteers donate countless hours. We all keep dreaming of new sources of financial support and new programs to help prisoners.

Heart Repairs

After Muriel's death, I found myself in an ocean of debt. When she was diagnosed with cancer, she was forced into immediate retirement. At that time, I had 23 men in the aftercare program and, without her income, I had little money to sustain the ministry. I was preoccupied with caring for her, so I did very little speaking, which was a secondary source of financial support. The Bishop encouraged Lutheran Family Services of Nebraska to help with prisoner programs, but after a few months, they knew it was not a program they could continue. My memory of those months after Muriel's death is very hazy. I was alone and turned to an old friend, alcohol. I needed to borrow money to keep the program alive, so I was falling deeper into debt.

On a Sunday afternoon in the late fall of 2005 I had a heart attack. I had scheduled a small home wedding for a former prisoner. As I was sitting in their living room waiting for the ladies to finish getting ready, I felt strange things happening inside. I suggested that we all sit through the wedding and stand for the vows. We did that, and when the brief wedding service was over, I excused myself and went to my church, Our Saviour's Lutheran. I took some aspirin and rested. That evening I had a meeting with some classmates at Nebraska Wesleyan to plan a skit, which we were scheduled to present in our Spanish class on Monday. After that meeting I went home to the cabin and slept through the night.

When I arrived at the prison for work on Monday morning, the officers at the front desk asked, "Are you all right?" I answered, "Yes, I think so. Why do you ask?"

They said, "Because you don't look so good. You look kind of grey."

I let that go and spent the day doing one-on-one visits with prisoners. Then I went out to the park to eat my supper. I had choir practice at the prison on Monday evenings. When the men arrived at the chapel, they took one look at me and said, "Something is wrong with you! We are not going to practice tonight." My volunteer accompanist agreed with the men. They insisted I go to the hospital to be checked out. They all went back to their units and I left for the hospital. When I arrived at the St. Elizabeth Emergency Room, the receptionist took one look at me and called for a wheelchair. They rushed me in for a checkup and called for a cardiologist. He scheduled surgery ASAP. Early that morning I had five by-passes.

My children were all concerned and thought one of them would have to come and stay with me. But before they could make any plans, I had a wonderful offer that I couldn't refuse. Samir and Amila Muslic, my friends from Bosnia, took me home with them and took care of me. I stayed in their lovely basement, and the whole family, including their children, Hana, Naila and Ema, ate meals with me in my temporary home. My family and I are forever grateful for their generosity!

That was the end of my work in the prison. The Bishop set in motion the process to call another pastor to take my place. I continued doing what I could for Bridges to Hope to raise a little money. The new prison pastor and volunteers did an amazing job of keeping everything going.

Interim Ministry

I am not the kind of person who can sit around and do nothing, even after heart surgery. I called the Bishop and told him I thought I might be able to do some work as an interim pastor. My first assignment was in Omaha at Luther Memorial Lutheran Church. They were surprised that an old guy like me with heart issues had so much energy. I really enjoyed my stay with them. It was close enough to my home at Horseshoe Lake so I could stay at home and commute to work.

My next assignment was St. Paul Lutheran Church in Auburn, Nebraska. Auburn was a little too far from home for the commute, so I brought a few items of furniture and stayed in the parsonage. The president of the congregation later told me he thought, "What can an old codger like him do for us?" But once again, time proved that I had lots of energy and lots of ideas for ministry. Three years went by very quickly, from my perspective. During my stay in Auburn, I married my new wife, Ruth.

While I was working in Auburn I was diagnosed with prostate cancer. The oncologist told me it was a very aggressive type of cancer and must be treated quickly. I agreed to have my prostate removed, and surgery was scheduled ASAP. It was Christmas time, and the earliest available date was the first part of January. When the day came, we were experiencing a severe winter storm. We managed to drive into Lincoln to the hospital, and Ruth found a motel room not far away. The doctor asked me how I would like to have the surgery done. I said, "Look, Doc, I don't know anything about such things. Do it the way you want to do it." He wanted to use the robot. It was new and he felt very comfortable, saying, "The robot's hands never shake!" The surgery went very well.

Because of the storm, some hospital workers didn't make it to work. The hospital was full and there was no room for me, so they put together a makeshift room at the end of the hall.

I got very sick and threw up all over my bed. I kept pushing the button, but nobody came. Later, I learned that I was allergic to morphine. I had a button to push when the pain got bad, so every time I pushed the button to give myself more morphine, I made myself sicker. Ruth came in the morning and everything was taken care of after she arrived. When the doctor came to check on me, I told him, "I'm ready to go home. I'm not getting very good care here and my wife is the best possible caregiver." He gave it some thought and finally agreed that I could go home. Meanwhile they had started giving me hydrocodone, and I suddenly became superman. Ruth said it was humorous to see me there in the hospital bed with all the tubes saying, "I can take care of that." We didn't tell the doctor that we couldn't go home because we had floor tilers there and our house was not available to us. We stayed at least a week at Mahoney State Park. I did well, even with my catheter, thanks to Ruth.

My next interim was in the beautiful village of Ponca, Nebraska. I thought to myself, it doesn't get any better than this. The people seemed to love the pageants I wrote for special occasions. The men were good singers, so we put together a men's chorus. We had our Christmas pageant on the coldest day of the year in a neighbor's barn/machine shed. I enjoyed two Husker banquets to raise money for prison ministry. Ponca was also too far for a realistic commute, so I stayed in the parsonage. I'll never forget driving into Ponca at Christmas time singing, "O Little Town of Ponca, How Still We See Thee Lie." The snow was falling softly, and it was a sight to behold snuggled among the hills of northeastern Nebraska.

One of my special Dad/Grandpa things happened in Ponca. My daughters, Nancy and Julie, and my granddaughter, Vanessa, came to sing at an outdoor community Memorial Day Service. Everyone was amazed by their singing and I was proud, proud, proud.

In Ponca I started to have issues with my heart again. It was gradually slowing down. When it got to about 40 beats per minute, Dr. Jain said we couldn't let this go any further. The doctors decided it was time to install a pacemaker. Ruth took me to the hospital in Lincoln. While we waited, she kept reminding me to "move my feet" to keep my heartbeat above 40. Soon I fell asleep and when I awoke, I noticed the monitor reported a steady 72 beats per minute. Every day since then I have been grateful for my pacemaker.

After Ponca came York, Nebraska. Again the people were wonderful and loved to participate in new things. My favorite memories of York have to do with the annual York Fest Parade. We made special t-shirts and built floats that took first place. Here we also did a lot of pageants. My favorite was a Christmas pageant in which Mary and Joseph told Jesus about his early life, and we re-enacted the scenes. My favorite scene was in the temple when Jesus was a young lad. One of our rabbis was an elderly blind man who played the part very well. My friend, Mark, came down from Ponca, and we made wonderful music together—Mark on the guitar, me on the piano, and my friend Dennis on the drums. Great memories.

Also while I was in York, my heart doctor gave me instructions to drink more liquids. He especially wanted me to drink Gatorade to combat my tendency to get dehydrated. I didn't do too well with that, partly because Ruth wasn't there to keep an eye on such things. My secretary kept a supply of Gatorade in the office, but I wasn't very diligent about drinking it. One Sunday morning while administering Holy Communion, I felt myself passing out. I quickly sat down on the front pew and threw up all over my robe. A wonderful retired doctor in the congregation immediately walked me to the car and took me to the hospital. On the way I told him, "We don't need to go to the hospital because I'm probably just dehydrated." He reminded me, "You are not the doctor now!" He was right, and I was right. They did all the usual tests and concluded that I was indeed dehydrated. After some IV treatment, I was sent home with instructions not to drive. However, it was Sunday afternoon and I "needed" to get home to my wife and to the lake. The drive home was no problem at all. The next Sunday Doc Loschen told the congregation, "Our pastor doesn't follow instructions well."

Finally, after York, I retired to spend time with my wife at our cabin by Horseshoe Lake. We keep busy with prison ministry and life is good.

Ruth

In the fall of 2006, I started a call as an interim pastor at Luther Memorial Lutheran Church in Omaha. In the fall of 2008, I finished my work there and received a new assignment in Auburn, Nebraska. When I was packing up to leave, I remember meeting Ruth in the hallway as I was carrying out the last of my office things. It suddenly occurred to me that I was really going to miss her. She was the organist and choir director at that time. I asked her if she would like to have dinner with me sometime. Her response sticks in my mind. She knew me well and said, "Yes, but there will be no alcohol." That was a perfect response.

Ruth and her husband Bob Hahn were both working at Luther Memorial when I started; Bob as the choir director and Ruth as the organist. Bob had leukemia, but he was a wonderful singer and amazed me more than once by getting up out of bed to sing a solo for a special occasion such as a funeral. I got to know him quite well. As his disease progressed, I had the opportunity to spend time with him in his hospital room. I always felt bad when I had to leave, because every time he awoke from a short nap, he checked to see if I was still there. One of the delightful parts of this not so delightful time was an opportunity to spend time with his daughter, Erin. She and her husband Paul live in Daytona Beach,

Florida. We didn't know that in a couple of years she would become my stepdaughter.

I also got to meet Ruth's son Tom and his wife Livia when they came home from Hungary for Bob's funeral.

Ruth and I were finally able to have dinner together on Valentine's Day, 2008. Shortly thereafter, she went on a trip to Hungary to visit her son and his family. Then she fell on the stairs at home and hurt her ankle, and I provided occasional transportation to see the doctor. Meanwhile, I received a call to do a three-year interim at St. Paul Lutheran Church in Auburn, Nebraska. Ruth and I continued to have dinner together and were married on June 25, 2009.

I remember the first time Ruth visited at Auburn. Three of the men came to me and said, "After worship we have to talk." I said, "O. K." I wondered what might be wrong. They were very solemn. They said, "We have been comparing notes and have decided that she is far too beautiful for an old guy like you."

Our wedding day was a wonderful day. We had most of the members of our families together at Our Saviour's Lutheran Church. Lee Griese, the Assistant to the Bishop and former pastor at Luther Memorial, officiated at our wedding. It was the beginning of a new life for me. Ruth moved into my lake cabin, and together we have been keeping track of the ducks and geese and cheering for the Kansas City Royals.

Ruth makes lovely quilts and I watch. Ruth paints pictures and I watch. Ruth makes delicious homemade soups, breads, and breakfast muffins and I watch. We take turns making treats to snack on. She was home alone a lot as I continued doing interim work at Salem Lutheran in Ponca, Nebraska, and at First Evangelical Lutheran in York.

We share many things in common. We both like to make music. We both enjoy cooking and baking. We both love nature and never tire of looking out at the lake and the ever-changing scene. We enjoy traveling, but we choose carefully where and when we go. I can't handle rugged terrain and high altitudes. We had traveled to Colorado early in our marriage, and the trip included a cog train trip up Pike's Peak. When we got to the top, I was as weak as a baby. I just sat on the bench until it was time to board the train for the trip down.

Ruth has to choose vacation sites that will not aggravate her asthma and allergies. We travelled to Michigan to visit Mackinac Island. I took the trip on the ferry to the island and Ruth stayed behind. We took a trip to Costa Rica, which we enjoyed very much, even though we both were sick for much of the time. We took a bus trip to New England to see the fall colors. We both agree: that was a great trip. We especially enjoyed the visit to the maple syrup farm and the boat ride to see the lobster fishermen in action. Our most recent trip was a bus tour from San Francisco down the California Coast to Los Angeles. We both enjoyed the rather long walk across the Golden Gate Bridge, the visit to Yosemite National Park, and the walking tour of the Haight-Asbury area of San Francisco.

Now, as the fall transitions into winter, we will spend some time browsing through travel brochures planning next year's trip.

Debts

I found doing interim ministry to my liking and enjoyed being back in parish ministry. I enjoyed getting the men out of the pews to sing in a men's chorus and writing pageants for special occasions like Christmas, Easter, Memorial Day, and Veteran's Day. Ruth was kind enough to join me in helping with music in the congregations I served.

Through the years since my heart attack, I have been working to pay off debts. The interim assignments made it possible. The debts accumulated because, after all these years, I'm still "irrepressible." For example, one debt is tied to the dining room at the lake place.

When I learned that Muriel was going to die of cancer, I immediately set out to fulfill some promises I had made when we bought our cabin by the lake. The biggest promise was a dining room. When we bought the cabin, there was a rickety old boat house/garage at the end of the house. Muriel had always wanted a dining room with a counter from which she could serve food when our family came home. My vision of what could happen "someday" was turning that space into a dining room because it was right off the kitchen.

By working late every night and with the help of my neighbors, we had the project completed in time for our Thanksgiving Dinner. By that time Muriel's health had deteriorated, but I could still talk everything over with her as I prepared a traditional Thanksgiving Dinner for our family: turkey, dressing, mashed potatoes, gravy, cranberries, scalloped corn, green bean casserole, yams, pies - we had it all! The best part for me was that Muriel was able to sit at the table with us in our new dining room. The counter was completely full of food, and we had room for everyone. A great memory!

The remainder of the debts were because of my determination to keep the Bridge program going. Muriel was the one who got it started, and I worked hard to keep it going in her honor. After my heart attack, my cardiologist told me I would have to simplify my life because I would need rest to recover. The houses and apartments were a big part of the expenses that were mounting up, and I knew I would have to give them up. I put them on the market with a realtor who was also my sponsor in AA. He did the best he could, but this all happened at the same time the bottom dropped out of the housing market. I sold both houses for less than I owed on them. I wondered, "How in the world will I ever be able to pay this?"

So, one difficult decision I made was to start spending the principal of "Muriel's Fund" (part of Freed for LIFE) to keep Bridges to Hope alive. I knew Muriel would not be happy in her heavenly home if I kept the money and let the program suffer.

Then, my son, Matt, and his wife, Monica, stepped up, took a second mortgage on their home, and extended me an indefinite loan at cost that cut my interest payments to something I could manage while attending to the rest of my debts. Likewise, a wonderful banker friend re-financed my cabin home for far more than it was worth, thus further cutting down on my interest payments.

When I added it all up, I was about $200,000 in debt. But God is good, and the help I received made it something I would eventually conquer. Since my surgery, my health has been good enough for me to keep working 15 years (and counting) past "retirement" age (65). I have systematically paid off the debt except for what I still owe on the house. And after all this, the prison ministry is in good hands and goes on. I have had prostate cancer surgery, received a pacemaker, and I, too, go on by the grace of God.

Now, in retirement, Ruth and I are content to let others do the "heavy lifting" while we do what we can to help tell the story and raise money. To God be the glory, great things God has done and is doing.

My Young Life

Now that I am 81 years old, and still canoeing, I sometimes think about things like, "How did I become the person I am today?" I know it has a lot to do with the family in which I grew up and with the experiences I have had along the way.

I was born at home like all of the twelve children in my family. My Aunt Julia came to act as midwife for her sister. Ma and Pa were pioneers, and they were both as tough as nails.

Ma (Inga) was born on April 9, 1898. She came from Norway in the early 1900's with her little sister, Julia. Ma was nine years old and Julia was seven, and they both worked as maids in the homes of the people who sponsored them. When they were fifteen, they were free to make their own way in this new country. They had older sisters and a brother who had come to America ahead of them, and so they went to Montevideo, Minnesota, to be with them. They both married at a young age and had large families.

Pa and Ma were married on October 16, 1915. They homesteaded in Wolf Point, Montana, living in a dugout home with their first son, Arthur. After a couple of years of bad weather and crop failures, they were forced to return to Minnesota. They farmed rental farms for many years until they were able to purchase forty acres. We still refer to that place as "the home place." I have five brothers and six sisters for a total of twelve children in our family. We lived in a small house that had a boys' room and a girls' room upstairs.

In picture above, there are two children missing from our family of twelve: My brother Clifford and my younger sister, Barbara. Barbara had not been born when this picture was taken, and Clifford died before I was born.

One sister, Elna, died shortly after giving birth to my niece, Marlys.

I was the eleventh child, so I lived at home with older parents who seemed more like grandparents. My older nieces and nephews were about the age of my younger sister and me. Some of my best memories of my childhood have to do with holidays when the family came home to the farm to celebrate Christmas or Thanksgiving.

We were a rather poor family, although we didn't know we were poor. There wasn't a lot of money for gift giving, so we always "chose names" and bought small gifts for the person whose name we drew out of a hat. Ma usually bought a box of bright red apples and kept them hidden in the basement until Christmas Day. She carried them up the stairs in her apron and shared them for an afternoon treat. The dinner was always a potluck dinner, but Ma provided the basics, usually home-grown chicken and roast beef with mashed potatoes and gravy. We had lots of pies for dessert.

After dinner, the older folks played cards. I usually got on an old pair of cross-country skis and went out across the fields to see what kinds of wildlife were out and about. We had a rifle, but early in my life I lost interest in killing rabbits and squirrels. I was always quiet and shy and felt much more comfortable by myself out in nature. To this day, even though people don't think of me as quiet and shy, I'm still most comfortable in the outdoors with my friends: the animals and the birds.

As a small boy I was always interested in water. We lived in Minnesota, the land of 10,000 lakes, but we seldom saw a lake. We stayed very close to the farm, working hard six days a week and resting on Sunday. Sometimes we would have company on Sunday afternoon after church. In the summertime the men would play horseshoes, and in the wintertime the adults would play canasta or whist.

Sunday was "play day" for me. We had a gravel pit in our pasture with a pond that we thought of as the neighborhood swimming hole. I was not allowed to go swimming unless my sister went with me because the water was deeper than my head and I didn't know how to swim. I did know how to dog paddle. At the end of a typical workday, children were forbidden to go near the gravel pit because young farm hands came there to cool off after working in the fields. It was common for five or six men to come skinny dipping. It didn't seem to bother anyone that the swimming hole was visible from the country road.

The only other water that I could get near was the shallow slough in our hog yard. I always dreamed of having a raft that I could stand on and push with a long pole. I tried my best to build one out of small willows, but my rafts seldom floated well enough to hold me. We had a pile of wooden fence posts that would have made a fine raft, but I was not allowed to use them. So I cut small willows and tied them together with vines. They seldom stayed together, and the best I could do was to lie flat on my back on the raft. The cool water felt good on my back, and it was a good place to watch the clouds moving overhead.

Most of the toys I played with as a child called for a good imagination. Usually they were rocks of various shapes. One was my truck, another my car, and another my tractor. The walls of the gravel pit had layers of clay, and I could dig out the clay with a stick and build a village as far in as I could reach. Once again, my

218

buildings were stones of various shapes. I was always on the look-out for special stones that looked like a barn, a corn crib or some other building.

I always wanted a pony. We had a horse named Babe that we would ride, but it wasn't like having a pony of my own. I was able to earn a little money helping at our neighbor's farm and eventually I saved $50. Pa told me they sold horses at the sale barn in Brookings where we bought and sold cattle. Finally, one day he said I could go along and look for a pony.

It was a long wait, watching pen after pen of cattle come into the sale ring. I had picked out a small black horse. I learned that the previous owner had named her "Black Beauty." There was no opportunity for me to ride her, but they assured me she was accustomed to being ridden. Pa talked to the owner, and they agreed that I could buy the horse for $50 without waiting for the sale. Pa was eager to get on the road home because we had cows to milk and it was getting late. We loaded the pony and headed for home. Of course, I didn't get to ride her because it was dark by the time we finished the chores. In fact, I had to wait until Sunday afternoon for my first ride.

Black Beauty was a perfect name. We had another horse named Beauty. She was a sorrel, so she became "Brown Beauty." Black Beauty was a feisty little animal. She loved to show her teeth and pretend she wanted to bite. When I came to the pasture to put her bridle on, she typically ran in circles around me two or three time before allowing me to catch her. I was accustomed to riding bareback. She came with a small saddle, which seemed like a nuisance to me. I wondered how she would respond to me sitting on her back without a saddle. She was fine.

Black Beauty and I spent many hours herding cattle in the road ditches around our farm. She had obviously been used as a cattle pony because she rounded up the cattle by herself. All I had to do was hang on because sometimes she turned quickly. Early on, I kicked her in the flanks to make her go and learned that was not a good idea. She reared up on her hind legs and I slid off her rump! No harm done. Mom was working in the garden nearby when it happened, and she got a good laugh out of my misfortune.

Ever since I was young, I have had an interest in Native American culture. Part of that interest came from an Indian hero named Straight Arrow. In my mind he was a perfect man, much like the Lone Ranger or other hero figures. Mom bought Nabisco Shredded Wheat, and I ate it even though it wasn't my favorite. Between the layers of shredded wheat biscuits were pieces of cardboard that featured Straight Arrow and Indian lore.

Straight Arrow taught me how to build a teepee, a travois, how to walk on snowshoes, and how to paddle a canoe. I have been practicing the art of paddling a canoe in a straight line for my whole life. From time to time people at the lake still ask me, and I'm happy to teach them what Straight Arrow taught me...to do the "J" stroke. I eagerly collected the cards and looked forward to the next box of shredded wheat.

My Baptism

Ma and Pa were devout Christians. They both came from Norwegian Lutheran families, so it was natural for us to be members of a small country parish near our home named Jevnaker Lutheran Church. When I was a child, most of the worship services were in Norwegian. Once a month we worshiped in English, and gradually we transitioned to English every Sunday. Reverend Jensen, the pastor when I was young, struggled a bit with English.

During the service, the men sat on the right side of the church and the women and children on the left. If we were having Holy Communion on a given Sunday, the men went to the sacristy to meet with the pastor. If they had something to "confess" to the pastor, they could do so. Otherwise they registered themselves and their wives and children who were confirmed and eligible to receive communion.

I was a sickly baby right after my birth. After about a month, Ma and Pa decided I was well enough for us to visit Aunt Julia and Uncle Gust. We had one car, a Model-A Ford, so we had to make two trips to transport the entire family. Art drove the car and took Ma and Pa and the younger children on the first trip and the older children on the second. On typical trips like this, Uncle Gust was ready with his barbering tools and each of the boys got a haircut. Then Aunt Julia served supper. The dining table was only big enough to seat the adults, so the children sat here and there at card tables.

On this particular visit, winter storm clouds began to gather, so Pa sent the older kids home to do chores. The plan was for Art to come back to pick up the rest of us, but the storm hit, and it was too dangerous for him to drive. We were stuck there at least for the night.

In the middle of the night, I became ill enough to worry Pa and Ma. There was no possibility of getting me to the doctor, so in the fear that I might not survive the night, they wanted me baptized. They did what was possible: Uncle Gust harnessed the horses, hitched them up to the bobsled, put fresh straw in the sled, and Aunt Julia got out blankets to cover us. Uncle Gust then drove the team along a fence line across the field to St. John's Lutheran Church with us in the back. In those days my parents called it a German Lutheran Church. Today we would call it a Missouri Synod Lutheran Church. I was baptized there in an emergency baptism.

The sequel to this story came years later when I was home on leave from the U. S. Navy. My sister, Ione, had married into that congregation, so I decided to accompany her one Sunday. I sat quietly in the pew while Ione did her duties as the Sunday School Superintendent. After a short while, the pastor came in to talk to Ione and informed her that the organist couldn't make it to church.

Ione said, "I'm sure my brother will be happy to play." I got a list of the hymns and found a few minutes to practice while Sunday school was in session. As I practiced, the pastor walked by and I quietly asked him if I could take communion with my sister. He said, "No. I think we would need more time to talk about it before I could give permission."

It was years later, at Ma's funeral, that I first heard the story of my baptism. As it turns out, I was baptized in the small baptismal font that stood right beside the organ I was playing for worship. (Church politics have never made much sense to me.)

Throughout my young life, this quotation was on the wall of my room.

"I can do all things through Christ, who strengthens me."

Philippians 4:13

This verse has been a constant source of comfort and encouragement for me.

Our Farm Home

Our farmhouse was built on the side of a hill. In the wintertime, it was a great hill for sledding. The bigger kids could start at the top and, if they could steer the sled to the right, they could slide from the top of the hill all the way down to the barn. I remember feeling a little cheated because I wasn't strong enough to steer to the right. They always had to stop me on the way down so I didn't veer off into our Model A Ford. The only way I could ride all the way down the hill was if I rode with one of my older siblings.

One summer day, the big "gravel pit machinery" moved onto our hill and started loading gravel trucks out of our back yard. The big hill disappeared and a new gravel pit appeared. It messed with our sledding hill but opened up a new play opportunity. The gravel was soft on our feet and we could jump off the "cliff," land in the soft gravel and slide to the bottom. We picked out all the stones so we didn't hurt our bare feet.

One Sunday afternoon I was out hiking around the farm. I enjoyed playing in the grove of trees behind our granary. Our farm dog, Terry, was a collie mixture. He watched the farm when we were gone, and he followed me around when I played alone in the grove. A rainstorm was brewing, and suddenly the wind started to blow and thunder and lightning accompanied a heavy downpour. To escape the storm, Terry and I crawled under the granary, and I soon fell asleep. I woke up to the calls of people hollering my name. Everyone was worried about me, and they were out searching. Terry answered their calls, giving away my location. I got a good scolding from Pa, but I knew Ma was relieved that I was safe.

I loved to play ball but didn't have anyone to play with except my sister. I had to bribe her to play by playing house with her first. We had a grove of trees down the hill from our house and marked off the walls of our pretend house with left-over twine from the wheat binder. My sister made all kinds of imaginary cookies, pies and cakes from mud - classic mud pies. When it was finally time to play ball, she always had to bat first. I would throw the ball to her and then chase down her hits. Occasionally I even caught one.

One of my vivid memories is the outhouse. It was located down in the grove not far from where we played house. We used an old Sears catalogue for toilet paper. I remember that the glossy pages didn't work very well, but all the softer pages were used up first. The trip to the outhouse was easy during the day, but nighttime was another matter. We didn't have flashlights and weren't allowed to use a lantern, so we used a candle. It was a scary adventure. Who knew what was out there in the dark?

My early life at home was lived under the shadow of World War II. It was just me, Ma and Pa, and two sisters, Arlene and Barbara, Three of my older brothers went into the military and all were assigned to the Pacific Theater. One of my most vivid memories is of Ma seated in her rocking chair late at night crocheting doilies, dresser scarfs, tablecloths and bedspreads. She was very quiet, and I knew she was praying for her sons.

We had no electricity or phone in the house, but we did have a battery powered radio so Ma and Pa could listen to the news about the War. From time to time, a neighbor family would get the news that one of their sons had been killed. I know that was a constant fear for many people. Finally, all three of my brothers came home safely. My oldest brother was shot in the head but managed to survive. He spent his entire life dealing with flash backs and would often wake from sleep screaming. I liked to look at the military medals they brought home, including purple hearts and silver stars.

Sometimes Ma and Pa would leave the radio on after the news and listen to the Beulah Show and/or Amos and Andy. It was one of the few things that made them smile.

Ma and Pa

Pa was a hard worker. Nothing could keep him from doing the important year-round tasks of feeding the animals, milking the cows, repairing fences, and grinding grain for feed. I remember a time when one of the horses kicked him. He had a broken rib and a cracked bone in his shoulder, but he still found a way to keep working.

Our farm was quite diversified. We raised corn, soybeans, sorghum, oats, flax, wheat and alfalfa. We raised beef cattle, dairy cows, hogs, chickens, geese, and ducks.

Ma worked equally hard. She crocheted beautiful, delicate doilies and milked ten cows with those same skillful hands. She never stopped gathering eggs. She raised a big garden. We had a large potato patch, a strawberry patch, and raspberry bushes. Ma and the kids all worked together in the garden.

Everyone had a job to do on the farm, and we all knew Ma was in charge. She assigned the tasks to each of us according to our age. Workstations were set up so we never ran out of things to do. Ma always had a quilt on the quilt rack so we could tie quilts. We had a small loom where we braided rugs from old clothing. She would send one of us down to the cooler to get fresh cream to shake butter. I don't remember having a butter churn. Ma put fresh cream in a two-quart jar, and we could shake it on our knees until butter started to form. Ma would keep a close eye on the new butter until it was ready. Then she would turn the chunk of butter out on the kitchen table to press the buttermilk out, adding just the right amount of salt.

The cooler was a small water tank between the well and the cattle tank. The cold well water passed through the cooler on the way to the cattle tank, so the water in it was always very cold. After the cows were milked, one of my tasks was to turn the cream separator. It had a hand crank, and when the separating was done, we took the skim milk to the house and dumped the cream into a large cream can in the cooler.

Ma didn't buy many things from the grocery store because we always had pantry and basement shelves filled with goods we had canned ourselves. Once a week, Ma and Pa went to town to sell the eggs and cream. The eggs were packed in 30 dozen crates. That provided money to buy staples like flour, sugar and salt.

Ma usually brought home a piece of candy for each of us. I remember orange slices, peppermints, horehound candy, and little "orange peanuts." My sisters and I would nibble on our piece of candy to see who could make it last the longest. I usually lost.

After the workday ended, Pa came in, washed up, and went to bed early. Ma patched our clothes or made "new" clothes for us out of old clothes or from the flour sacks. I can picture her studying the flour sacks made of fabric with a variety of designs and envisioning what she could make from them. She made dresses and blouses for the girls and very nice shirts for me. Still, I was a little embarrassed when I had to wear homemade stuff to school. I remember shirts made out of the backs of Pa's worn out chambray shirts, with sleeves and pockets made of some other fabric. Those shirts would have been in demand today. Of course, as a child in elementary school, I didn't want to look different.

Autumn

For me, autumn was the best time of the year on the farm. It was payday for farmers. The work of harvesting was difficult but rewarding. It was the time we got to reap the results of a long spring and summer of planting and cultivating. The fertilizer we spread on the fields came from the manure pile behind the barn and the bottoms of rotting straw pile. We loaded the manure spreader by hand with four- or five-tined forks.

We didn't spray weeds with herbicides. We planted the corn in hills and cultivated both directions to keep the weeds under control. It was a sign that I was growing up when Pa asked me if I thought I could cultivate corn. Of course, I said, "Yes." He took me to the field, set me on the tractor and told me to keep the corn plants between the spacers. It took some practice, but I went slowly at first so I didn't plow out the corn. It was a challenge to stay alert in the hot summer sun. The sound of the tractor droned on and on, and the sight of the corn plants passing between the spacers was mesmerizing. It was safe for me to sing while cultivating corn because the tractor made enough noise so Pa couldn't hear me.

The other thing we did to control weeds was walk the fields and pull them. We pulled the mustard plants out of the bean fields. Pulling out thistles was a never-ending job.

The earliest grain to be harvested was the small grain. That included oats, wheat, barley, and flax. Pa and my older brothers drove the binder that cut the crop and tied it into bundles. My job was to come behind the binder and stack the bundles into "shocks" of six bundles. Oats was the easiest to shock because it didn't have any beards. Wheat and barley beards clung to our sweaty skin and made us itch and scratch.

The threshing machine was fascinating to watch. It had lots of moving parts: rocker arms, pulleys, chains and belts. My older brother, Art, was in charge of the threshing crews in our neighborhood. The farmers met at our house and determined whose fields would be first. Art slowly moved the machine from one field to another. It was top heavy, and the fear was that it might tip on uneven ground. When he got it to the location where the farmer wanted his straw pile, he greased every moving part. Then he set the old Alice Chalmers tractor in the proper place so the long drive belt wouldn't fly off when the threshing machine got up to speed.

Hauling bundles was a job that I eventually grew into. Loading the hayrack with bundles was a work of art. The object was to load a nice square rack full and move it up alongside the threshing machine without losing any bundles. We were afraid that someone might get hurt while unloading bundles into the threshing machine. If we fed the machine too fast, it would clog.

Then my brother had to stop the whole operation and unplug the machine by hand.

My earliest assignment during threshing time was hauling the wagons full of grain to the granary. The challenge was to back the wagon up to the elevator without having to go forward and back several times until you got it right. It was intimidating to have my older brothers standing by watching.

Another job that the neighborhood did together was filling the silos. My cousin owned and operated the silo filler. Each farmer cut and bundled as much green corn as he needed to fill his silo. The farmers all came with their hayracks to haul the bundles to the silo. Then the silo filler was set up and the silage was chopped and blown into the silo. Someone had to be in the silo to distribute the silage evenly as it came through the blower. It was not where I wanted to be even though I liked the smell of fresh silage.

For me, the best part of harvest was the lunches and snacks the women prepared. We always took a break mid-morning and another mid-afternoon. That was when we had coffee, sandwiches, and cookies or cake. The best part was the noon hour. We had a bucket of cold water and soap for everyone to wash up. Then we sat down to eat the most wonderful meals you can imagine: chicken or roast beef, mashed potatoes and gravy, vegetables, fresh rolls, and a variety of homemade pies. Those meals tasted best when we were working hard.

Potato picking was a very important activity in our neighborhood. Potatoes were the staple in our diet. You can't make lefsa without potatoes. Children were excused from school when it was time to dig the potatoes. We turned the plants over, picked up the potatoes, and carried them in bushel baskets to the cellar beneath our house.

We put carrots in a crock filled with sand to keep them moist as long as possible. Our neighbors gave us apples from their tree. These were wrapped individually in brown paper or newspaper and stored in boxes. Mom called them cooking apples, but to me they were pie apples. Ma also canned some crab apple pickles.

Every fall Pa sold a steer to have money to buy fruit that we didn't raise on the farm. When the fruit came into the grocery store, Ma and Pa went to town to buy lugs of peaches, pears, apricots, and plums. Ma canned sauce and made preserves until our cellar shelves were full.

Another fall activity that fascinated me was butchering. I was not allowed to be around when a hog or a steer was killed. Pa killed the animal, gutted it and hoisted it up in a tree. The blood was caught in a small tub and had to be stirred until it cooled. That was a job for one of the kids. Ma sewed some cloth sacks, thickened the blood with flour, spiced it up a bit, added some salt pork chunks and spooned it into the sacks. She sewed the end shut and put the filled sacks into boiling water. My job was to carry water from the well to fill the big copper boiler that stood on the kitchen cook stove. My next job was to feed the cook stove with corncobs. The blood sausage was cooled, sliced and fried in butter. We ate it with syrup. We also cut it into chunks and heated it in a cream sauce. We thought it was a great treat.

Ma and Pa brought the carcasses of the hog or steer to the kitchen where Ma cut it up. We didn't have electricity so there was no placed to store the meat. Ma cut it up and canned it, usually in two-quart jars. The shelves in the cellar where filled with jars of pickles, sauce, vegetables, and meat. If company came, it was relatively easy for Ma to prepare dinner. She would send me to the cellar with a list of things to bring up to the kitchen.

A treat we looked forward to every year was pickled pigs' feet. Ma also made some salt pork. Nothing was wasted. Ma boiled the head of the hog and made head cheese to be used as sandwich meat or to be eaten with vinegar. She also made *rulepulsa* from the flanks. She covered the meat with appropriate spices, rolled it, and tied it with a string. It was then cooked, cooled, and sliced to be eaten on sandwiches.

Every year we purchased baby chickens. Some chicks were raised to become laying hens, and 100 rooster chicks were raised to provide fresh chicken meat. The rest of the chicks, when they were grown, were canned and placed in the cellar for winter.

Ma also raised ducks and geese. Some of our laying hens wanted to keep their eggs and raise a family of chicks, but Ma would fool them by stealing their eggs and replacing them with goose eggs or duck eggs. These were eggs we stole from the nests we found near the pond in the hog pasture. When the baby ducks or geese hatched, it was common to see a mother hen roaming the yard with the new babies. Then the day would come when they found their way to the pond in the hog yard, and mama hen had to be satisfied to stand on the shore while she watched her babies

234

swim away. It amazed me that each one knew his or her own mother. When we had enough eggs for the cluck hens, we let the ducks and geese keep their eggs to raise their own family.

To protect the baby chicks, ducks, and geese, we turned the bottom of a triple box (wagon box) upside down and built a small fenced enclosure to keep them in. One morning Ma came out to feed the ducklings and saw a chicken hawk snacking on one of the ducklings. She hit it over the head with a board and killed it. However, it really wasn't a chicken hawk. It was a Great Horned Owl. I put it in a bag and took it to the biology teacher at our high school. He, an amateur taxidermist, mounted the owl on a branch to keep in the science room.

Our Country Church

As tough a pioneer as Ma was, she was also a very tender-hearted lady. I was a rather weak and sickly child, and I realized later that she probably worried that she might lose me like she had lost my brother Clifford. I had a lot of pain in my legs, and later in life I learned that I probably had a light case of polio. In those days before WW II, the polio epidemic had not yet hit, so our local doctors didn't know much about it. Ma found ways to entertain me to take my mind off the pain.

One way she entertained me was to carefully teach me how to cook and bake. One of my favorite memories is when she taught me to make peanut cake. I stirred up the cake batter according to her instructions and put the cake in the oven. When it was baked to Ma's satisfaction, we cooled it and cut it into pieces. My task was to sit at the kitchen table and frost all six sides of each piece while she worked at other things. We rolled the frosted pieces in crushed peanuts. To this day it is one of my favorite things to do. On a stormy winter day, you may find me at the island in the kitchen of our home by the lake making peanut cake.

Ma was also the teacher in our family. Even though she had a very limited education herself, she knew the basics. She taught all of her children Peterson's *Explanation to Luther's Small Catechism*. I'm sure she knew it by heart. When it was my turn to "read for the minister," Pa picked up several of the neighborhood children and took us to the country church to meet with Reverend C. T. Jensen. I was always a little afraid of him because he spoke broken English, but perfect Norwegian. Although we never dared to talk about it, we knew that he smoked cigars. I didn't dare go to class without knowing my lesson perfectly. On a typical Saturday we learned one of the commandments, several Bible verses, and five or six explanatory answers. Mom had me recite the question and then give the answer. The end result was that I knew the whole book by heart, including all the questions.

Small for my age, I was about half the size of my classmates. We usually attended catechism classes for two years, but at the end of my first year the pastor came to talk with my parents. He said I knew the material so well, thanks to Ma, there was really no need for me to come for the second year. In my confirmation picture, I look like a second grader alongside the other eighth graders who had finished in two years. In those days we also had catechization on Sunday morning before confirmation day. We lined up in front of the congregation to demonstrate what we had learned. Of course, thanks to Ma, I was the star of the show. If nobody else knew the answer, I did.

The church was the center of our social life. People went to church to worship, and to meet and socialize with our neighbors. The women were well organized into "circles" that met monthly for Bible Study. The men not so much. The women were ready to serve lunch for funerals, farms sales, and any other community function.

The youth of the congregation met once a month on a Sunday evening for Luther League. Everyone came to Luther League night. The youth had their business meetings upstairs in the sanctuary. Meanwhile, the adults met in the basement for coffee. Coffee meant another small meal with open faced sandwiches, jello and cake.

Everyone took good care of the cemetery plots of family members who had died. Other plots of people who didn't have any family nearby were also cared for. There was no need for an organized plan to take care of the cemetery because everyone knew what needed to be done. We all loaded up our push mowers and clippers (in those days there were no motorized lawn mowers or weed whackers). Memorial Day was commonly called Decoration Day. Everyone brought flowers and flags to decorate the cemetery, and families made trips to several cemeteries to visit the graves of loved ones.

Cleaning the church building was a task everyone shared. We had no custodian, but the building was always clean. Families were assigned to clean the church on a rotating basis. Women did most of the cleaning. White gloves were kept behind the altar to wear while working in the chancel area. The brass was polished even if it didn't seem to need it. This was an act of devotion.

Family Life

Both Pa and Ma were intolerant of complaining. They had been through hard times, survived the loss of their homestead, buried two children, and lived through the Dirty Thirties and WWII. I never wanted to act like I was bored because Ma would set me down at the kitchen table with a red tablet and have me make a list of things I was thankful for. If my pump needed to be primed, she would make some suggestions to get me going. One I remember and smile about to this day is, "the breeze that blows away the bugs while we are picking raspberries." She often said, "Little things mean a lot." I find myself saying that to my family and friends.

Because I was small for my age, I always felt I was a disappointment to my parents. I knew better than to say, "I can't," because Ma would interrupt with, "There's no such word as 'can't.' It may take you a little longer, but you can get it done." My brothers would pick up a gunny sack full of feed for the hogs and carry it on their shoulders to the hog feeders. I had to put the sack in the wheelbarrow, fill it with a can, wheel it down to the hog house and empty it with the can. Pa expressed his frustration with me by saying, "You will never be a farmer."

Pa had a plan in mind to help each of his sons get a jump start on their lives. His plan was to purchase five 80-acre plots of land to be sold to each of us in turn when the time was right. All we had to do was pick up the loan payments. Times changed, however, and by the time we got old enough to farm the land, eighty acres was too small. He did manage to get the land and eventually turned it over to each of us in turn. I told him I really didn't need the land because I had a college education, a seminary education, and a livable income. However, before he died, he insisted that I take over the eighty that was designated for me. I was a pastor in Brooklyn at the time, so my older brother farmed the land. When Pa died, I turned it over to my brother in the same way I had received it.

It was Pa's expectation that the girls would meet a man and get married. Their husband was responsible to take care of them. Pa and Ma bought each daughter a cedar hope chest which they could fill with hand-made things for their future home. For their wedding gift, the girls got a bedroom set. That hardly seems fair compared to an eighty-acre plot of farmland.

Pa seldom showed any emotion. He was the living demonstration of what it means to be stoic. He seldom showed any anger, even when I knew he was angry. As a child I enjoyed making a sling shot and shooting rocks at fence posts and other things. Pa had some rules that he expected me to follow. Never shoot at the farm animals. Never shoot the sling shot in the farmyard. I could shoot in the gravel pits and along the road when I was herding the cattle. One day I was bringing the cattle home for milking and thought, "I will just shoot one more shot." I shot at a bird on the electrical wire that crossed over our yard. I missed the bird, as I always did, and hit the barn window instead. I was scared and broken hearted. I didn't say a word as we milked cows, but I looked at Pa to see if there was any evidence on his face that he knew about the window. There was no expression. I found myself getting angry with him because I thought he wasn't saying anything just to make me suffer. After supper we went to bed and I tried to sleep, but it was difficult. The next morning we got up early to do chores and milk the cows again. I found myself blurting out, "I broke the barn window with my sling shot!" He walked to the kitchen window, looked out and said, "Crawl up the ladder and board it up. Next time it rains we will fix it." We will fix it! And we did. What a gracious thing to say. I felt so much better, getting it off my chest.

Ma was a tough but tender parent. In my first year in elementary school, we were walking home from school one day and I complained that my siblings were walking too fast for me to keep up. I got upset and set my dinner pail (a syrup pail) down by the mailbox and ran to keep up. Of course they told Ma immediately and I knew I was in trouble. She said, "Do your chores and then you can go back to get it." Again, I complained that it would be dark by the time I got my chores done, but she just ignored me. I rushed to get my chores done and then it was time to go back for the dinner pail. She walked with me to the end of our driveway and sent me on my way. I was scared, but I kept walking, crying to myself. I knew I couldn't turn around and go back home without my dinner pail. Finally, I picked up my syrup pail and ran home through the dark. As I topped the hill, half-way home, I could see through the darkness that Ma was still at the end of the driveway waiting for me. She complimented me on my bravery and called me her "little man." Now I think back to her busy schedule. She was able to set it aside while she waited for me.

We had relatively few rules to live by in our family. The best way to stay out of trouble was to work hard. There was little time for play. One of the rules was that we were to stay out of the parlor. Even though our house was small, we only used the parlor when company came, usually on Sundays. In the parlor sat an old *Shoninger* piano that was of great interest to me. When everyone was outside working, I would sneak into the parlor and play the piano very softly. I had no teacher, so I learned to pick out tunes by ear. Gradually I discovered chords. Certain keys sounded good together. By the time I was five years old, I could play some tunes, especially country music and songs we called "Old Time" tunes. I also learned to play the songs we sang in Sunday School. Eventually, I learned that Ma knew my secret, probably because my sisters told her. Pa was always out working, so he didn't know.

One day we had company and everyone was in the parlor visiting. During a lull in the conversation, my sister said, "Bud, why don't you play the piano?" I was surprised. Everyone was surprised, but she went on, "Play Golden Slippers." That was ingenious because we all knew it was Pa's favorite. I played it and he smiled and tapped his feet. My secret was out...and it was OK! My older siblings could remember that Pa played the violin before he cut off his finger in the small corn sheller, but I have no memory of Pa's musical talents.

People said to my parents, "You should give him piano lessons." I thought that would be too expensive, but Ma arranged for me to go to a piano teacher when they brought the eggs and cream to town each Saturday. It cost fifty cents for a lesson, so when they sold the produce, they gave me a shiny half dollar. That was a lot because they only had seven or eight dollars to buy flour, sugar, and salt.

After a few lessons it was time for a recital. I had no shoes to wear, so my sister, who worked downtown at the Sugar Bowl (a small restaurant), took me to the S & L store and bought me a pair of moccasins for two dollars. That seemed extravagant to me. The teacher assigned a piece called, "The All is Rosy Polka," for me to learn. It didn't take long for me to learn it and then I started to spice it up a little with my own variations. When I played for my teacher one last time before the recital, I accidentally included some of my own notes. She stopped me and said, sternly, "Please! Just play what's on the page!"

I never got over feeling guilty about spending our food money for piano lessons. I told Ma and Pa that I really didn't want to take any more piano lessons, so they let me quit. However, I never finished picking out tunes on the piano for myself. Recently, one of my grandchildren asked me, "Grandpa, how many songs do you know?" I said, "I don't know. How many songs can I hum?"

Growth Spurt

The bane of my childhood was that I was a bed wetter. I think it would be fair to say that I hated myself because of it. We didn't have indoor plumbing, but I tried hard to keep myself clean. Every day while I was doing chores, I would sneak behind the hay pile with a pail of cold water to clean myself up before school. Sometimes I would wash my bedding by hand and hang it on the line. There was no way to keep any of this secret. Everybody in my family knew about it, and all of my classmates knew. Being very small was bad enough but being a small bed-wetter made everything worse.

My folks tried everything. They tried to shame me into quitting this disgusting habit. They tried scolding me. They took me to the doctor and he prescribed cod-liver oil. Yuck!

This didn't end until I experienced a growth spurt in my sophomore year in high school. When I passed my driver's license exam, the examiner said, "I'm going to put five foot two inches for your height because you will no doubt grow." I was four feet eleven inches tall and weighed about eighty pounds. When I went back to school for the start my senior year just a year and a half later, I had grown to five feet nine inches, and by the end of that year I was five feet eleven inches. My driver's license still said five foot two.

I played bus league basketball at noon. Country kids rode to school on buses, and each bus had a basketball team. One day, the basketball coach came to watch our game and was impressed by my ability. After the game, he asked me if I was a new freshman, hoping that he had found a future varsity player. I said, "No, I'm Bud Christenson. I'm a senior. I was in your social studies class last year." He was surprised, and I think a little disappointed.

I worried for a long time that the bed-wetting might return. I went off to college and shared an apartment with six other young men. I worried every night. After two years, I joined the U. S. Navy and worried. Finally, I concluded that it was something that was behind me and would not come back to haunt me, although at times it still haunted my dreams.

I experienced my share of bullying as a child in school. As I look back, it turned out to be a blessing because I became very sensitive to the problems of other people. I learned to dislike bullies, and it became my passion to try to stop them wherever I saw them in the act. When I became a street pastor in Brooklyn, I found lots of abused children to walk and talk with and care for. Throughout my years in the ministry I have been known as someone who truly cares for those who are needy or less fortunate in some way.

High School and College

The expectation in my family was that each child would graduate the eighth grade from the country school. The girls could go on to high school, but it was generally thought that the boys should stay home and work on the farm. Two of my sisters went to high school, and I dearly wanted to go too. I detected a little disgust in Pa's voice when he said, "You might as well, because you will never be a farmer."

I went to high school and did very well, academically, but I was intimidated by the town kids. My anxiety caused me to develop a stutter that further embarrassed me. I was an easy target. I tried to fit in, but I thought it was a lost cause. My self-image was pretty low. I wished I could go out for sports, but we lived too far from town and transportation was a problem. The only extra thing I could do was sing in the choir because rehearsal was during the school day. I never felt much support from home because my folks didn't go to town unless it was absolutely necessary.

I remember one wonderful teacher who seemed to understand me. She taught speech and, until I met her, I was afraid of getting up in front of people. She recognized an ability in me that I didn't recognize. Nobody else recognized it, either. She encouraged me to take a small part in the class play.

Throughout high school I felt like I was invisible. As we entered our senior year, the counselor was calling students in to talk to them about college and potential scholarships. Even though my grades put me near the top of our class, no one talked to me about going to college. I was almost afraid to bring it up at home because Pa would think I "was just trying to get out of work." My sister was a student at St. Cloud State studying to be a teacher. I thought it would be easy for us to travel together since I had a car. She said we could offer rides to other students on the weekend and that would pay for our gas. I knew it would cost $100 a year for tuition, and I needed money for books and room and board.

I finally brought up the subject at home and was surprised by the response of Pa and Ma. Ma, of course, was excited about sending me to college. Pa was reserved, but willing to go along with the plan.

I roomed with six other men in the upstairs of a private home. The apartment had two bedrooms, a kitchen and a bathroom. Four men shared the bigger bedroom and three shared the smaller one. It cost us each four dollars a week for rent and four dollars a week for food. We took turns shopping, cooking, and doing clean-up. It worked out surprisingly well. I was fortunate to get the single bed. The other men slept two to a bed. The landlords, Mr. and Mrs. Burnett, invited us to share their TV room every evening. There was only one functional channel, so we watched things like the Lawrence Welk Show.

College was the first time in my life that I felt respected and appreciated. I was a good typist so I typed my roommates' papers. I also helped them write their papers because I knew about complete sentences and paragraphs. They were rugged veterans and heavy drinkers, but they were all nice to me.

Dale was my favorite roommate. He had been in the Sea Bees in the U. S. Navy. The Navy trained him to be an auto mechanic, so he knew things I didn't know. I could type his papers, and he could fix my car. We became good friends. He invited me to come home with him to Minneapolis one weekend, and his brother, a pilot, took me up in a Piper Cub for my first airplane ride. He also invited me to go camping and canoeing one weekend and taught me about canoes. He was an avid outdoors person like me. Later, he was a groomsman at my wedding and we maintained our friendship throughout his life. He fulfilled his dream by becoming a Social Studies teacher in northern Minnesota. He raised some cattle for a hobby and spent his extra time hunting, fishing and trapping. He became a role model for me in many ways.

My dream in life was to get away from people by working in the country. I studied conservation and dreamed about working in the forests, clearing hiking trails, and taking care of trees and animal life. I met my future wife in college and learned that she loved nature as much as I did. Together we dreamed about teaching in a small town, living on a farm, raising a few cattle, and running a tree farm.

Muriel

I met Muriel during freshman orientation week. She was an obvious leader and seemed to be involved in everything. I was a bit shy and stayed in the background. In the course of get-acquainted conversations led by senior camp counselors, it was revealed that I had been a cheerleader in high school. They didn't know I had missed most of the games. Nevertheless, because I could "tumble" a bit, I was voted on to the cheerleading squad. There was always a need for "yell kings." Girls had to be good to make the squad. Boys just had to be male. Games became a natural meeting place for Muriel and me because she played in the band and I was out on the field, or the floor, leading cheers. She always asked me for a ride to and from the games, and I was happy to provide it. Often, after a game, I would go with her to Lawrence Hall, the girls' dorm, and play the piano for an impromptu sing-along. Our friendship grew. There was no money for dating, but we met in the library to study. If we had a dime to spare, we shared a coke, "with two straws, please," at Almy's, a small store on campus. Muriel was a great student, full of confidence and seemed to know everything about the library. I leaned on her knowledge, and her confidence, to help me find my way around the library and around campus.

Despite this budding relationship, it turned out that I needed to get away to give myself time to grow up and get over some of my fear of the future. I had a secret dream that one day I might become a fighter pilot. That never happened, but one day during my sophomore year, I was working at home with Pa on the farm and he sent me to town to get parts to repair one of the machines. On the way home, I stopped in at the Navy recruiter's office and signed up. It seemed like a spur of the moment thing, but I had been thinking about military service ever since my brothers came home after WWII.

Muriel and I were "going steady" by that time, and she was very angry when she found out that I had enlisted. She announced to me and her friends that she was not going to wait around for four years. I was disappointed, but I respected her feelings. I told her I was going to wait until I knew for sure there was no future for our relationship. I went to boot camp and was assigned to a surveyor school in the U. S. Navy Sea Bees. That made me happy because I was following the steps of my buddy, Dale. I graduated first in my class and had my choice of duty assignments. I chose to go to the Hydrographic Survey Ship, the USS Tanner, because I was told if I spent my first two years on sea duty there was a good possibility I could spend the remaining two years on shore duty. I still had not given up on my hopes that Muriel might change her mind.

One day during surveyor school, I received a wonderful letter from her informing me that she had changed her mind. She had tried dating a couple of college students, but I was always on her mind. She finally decided she would wait for me, finish her college, degree and get a job teaching.

With this renewed hope, I went to the Navy Exchange to see how much diamond rings cost. I found one that seemed perfect for us, set it aside, and started making payments on it. When I finished school and was preparing to head for my ship in the Mediterranean, I was given a ten-day leave. I put the ring in the glove compartment of my car thinking I would keep it there until I felt sure that we were still right for each other. I drove to St. Cloud to see Muriel, and I knew immediately what I would do. The first evening we spent together, I asked her to marry me. There was a look of panic on her face and her first question was, "When?" I said, "Sometime in the future when I earn more leave time." I assured her there was no hurry. She said an enthusiastic, "Yes," and couldn't wait to get back to her dorm to share the news and show off her new ring. Wow! That is a happy memory!

Muriel did finished college, got a job teaching, and started making plans for our wedding someday in the future. Then, during my second year on the ship when we came back to our home port in Brooklyn, some of my shipmates gave up some of their leave time so I could have ten days and get married (each crew member got a short leave because we didn't have much time before our next cruise). We were married on December 28, 1958, at her home church in Wadena, Minnesota. We spent our honeymoon, according to her plan, at her apartment.

During the wedding, our car was decorated with lots of soap writing, so one of the first things we had to do after the wedding was wash the car. We laughed and laughed because it was very cold and the soap suds that we produced kept freezing. We didn't have money to go to a car wash in those days so we just kept washing until we got the job done. We carried bucket after bucket of hot water from the apartment to the parking lot. What a mess! And what fun!

After our wedding, Muriel went back to teaching and I had to go back to my ship - but suddenly I wanted out of the Navy! It helped that we wrote letters every day, even though I couldn't receive her letters or mail my letters more than about once a week. It was fun getting six or seven letters every time we had mail call. Some of my shipmates were jealous.

USS Tanner

At the start of my regular duty as a surveyor in the U.S. Navy, I needed to catch my ship, the USS Tanner, in Turkey. I had a long layover in the Brooklyn Navy Yard while I waited for a crew ship to take me overseas, so I was assigned to work as a short order cook in the Navy *Gedunk*, a snack bar. One of my memories of that job was of the elderly retired admiral who came in every morning. He always wanted eggs over easy, and I mean easy. They barely touched the grill and he would say, "That's enough!" He liked his eggs nearly raw and his toast dark brown. If they weren't just right, we had to start over.

I rode a crew ship overseas with a group of soldiers who were heading for assignments in Europe. It was a very slow trip, and when we finally arrived in Rome, I was directed to a cargo plane that would take me to a Naval Air Station in Turkey. I didn't have any orders in my hands, so I was totally dependent on others to tell me what to do and where to go. The Office at the Air Station arranged for a Jeep ride to take me to the nearest port to wait for my ship. The ship was "running lines" offshore, so I could see it from a distance. I was told a boat would come for me soon, "So, stay on the pier." I waited all day, but the boat didn't come. It was getting dark when a Jeep finally returned to pick me up and take me back to the airbase. Finally, on the third day, an LCVP (Landing Craft, Vehicle, Personnel) came, the crew called out my name, and I climbed aboard. When we got to the ship, I climbed up a rope ladder and entered a new and very strange world. I had been warned that the crew loved to play games with new crew members, so I expected the worst. I didn't fall for the order to go pick up three feet of "chow line." By the way, "line" is the sailors' way of saying rope.

It was a relief to be assigned to a bunk and have an opportunity to meet my new shipmates in the Hydrographic Department. My first assignment was to do kitchen duty (KP). I thought to myself, "I'm trained to be a surveyor. What am I doing here in the kitchen?" But, I learned that this was a routine that new crew members had to endure. I didn't waste any time preparing to take the test to become a third-class petty officer. That meant a small raise in pay, but more importantly, no more KP.

When my KP was over, I joined other surveyors to learn about our job. We were in charge of drawing up "boat sheets" with lines for the ship to follow. A surveyor plotted our ship location on the chart and gave directions to keep us on the line. At the same time, others were reading the fathometer, which gave us the depth of the water while we plotted the location. Later, these boat sheets were converted into smooth sheets that became the source of information for new ocean charts.

While the ship was running lines in deeper water, the "sound boats" were running lines in the shallow water near the shore. At the same time, the photographers in our division were taking pictures of the shoreline from helicopters. The pictures were superimposed on the smooth sheets to create as accurate a picture of the shoreline as possible.

While this was going on, other surveyors were at shore stations (camps) locating points on the top of mountain peaks where we could set up towers for SHORAN (short range navigation) and LORAC (long range navigation) electronic stations that would send out signals. Triangulation networks allowed us to locate the ship moment by moment as we ran lines.

I was happy to work anywhere. I enjoyed setting up 75-foot Bilby Towers on the tops of the mountains. I enjoyed duty on the sound boats. I enjoyed "conning" the ship to keep it on line. I enjoyed working in the drafting room. Unfortunately, after people got to know my ability to type, I had an assignment that kept me away from these tasks. I was the only one on the ship who could operate the linotype machine. It was a fancy typewriter on which I would type one line at a time, proofread it, and then push the button and it would type the perfect copy. We had men on board who were trained printers, but this machine replaced the hand setting they would do. None of them knew how to type.

Because I was willing to sacrifice my surveyor preferences to do this typing, I received a recommendation for what was called "proficiency pay." That meant I could take the test for First Class Petty Officer, and even though I didn't have enough time-in to wear the stripes, I got the first class pay. It wasn't much, but it helped.

After getting married, I would listen carefully to the "scuttlebutt" (rumors) about when we might be back home because I knew our next stay would be in dry dock. That meant we would be home longer and, if it were summer, Muriel could come to stay with me for a few weeks. When it finally happened, she came to stay with me in Brooklyn. The tiny apartment we rented was in the neighborhood near the shipyard where we were docked. Muriel went to work on the apartment while I was busy on the ship. She scrubbed every inch of the apartment, the hallway, the bathroom we shared with other tenants, and all the furniture. On Sunday morning we walked to a nearby church to attend worship. On the way, we met an elderly woman who stopped, looked us up and down, and exclaimed, "My...you look so...clean!" I remember I was dressed in my navy-blue suit and Muriel was dressed in a summery yellow dress with white cuffs on the short sleeves. I think we really did look "clean" in comparison to our surroundings.

After a week or so, we learned that we would be moving to dry dock in Hoboken, New Jersey, so we moved to there. Again, we found a tiny apartment with an old-fashioned gas stove in the kitchen. Again, Muriel scrubbed every inch of the apartment, the furniture, the hallway, and the bathroom we shared with other tenants. We could smell "the clean" when we walked into the hallway in front of our apartment. One other tenant actually thanked us. That was a surprise, because most people in New York didn't talk to strangers.

An ice-cream shop stood on the corner a couple of blocks from our apartment. Every evening we walked there to get a ten-cent cone. What a treat! I'm not sure which was the better treat, the ten cent cones we shared or the park bench we sat on. It was a park bench without a park, but that didn't matter to two kids in love.

During this time, Muriel and I used my extra pay to buy a new Volkswagen, for which we paid $1,500 cash. We had some Pennsylvania Dutch friends who would say to us, "Remember, it is 'younst' (your) turn to come visit us." So Muriel named our new Volkswagen "Ounst" (Ours) in their honor.

After our stay in dry dock, we were scheduled for a "shake down" cruise to Cuba. It was a trip to test the work that had been done on the ship. When I first came on board the USS Tanner, we had some gun turrets on the ship. The ship had been a cargo ship during World War II and was converted to a hydrographic survey ship after the war ended. We didn't need the guns so they had been removed to make room for other things. The ship was very old, having been built in 1936 (the year I was born). Now it was overloaded with a much bigger crew, two helicopters on the aft flight deck, four fifty-two-foot sound boats, a captain's gig (private boat), a crew liberty boat, two LCVPs, a DUKW (an amphibious vehicle for land and water), and several 6X6 trucks. Our cruising speed was seven knots. Flank speed (maximum) was thirteen knots, but the ship felt like it would break apart at that speed so we didn't go that fast. On the trip to Cuba we had a short stop in Ft. Lauderdale, Florida. That was the occasion for another short "vacation" visit for Muriel. We spent my time off walking on the beach, catching up on our lives apart, and dreaming about the future when I would come home to stay.

USS Tanner

Life on the Ship

After the "shake down" cruise to Cuba, we went back to the Eastern Mediterranean to complete our work. These cruises were usually seven to nine months in length. We had a ten day stay in port somewhere halfway through the cruise. One liberty port was Naples, Italy. Another time we had a stop in Athens, Greece. In Italy I went shopping for an accordion. First I bought a smaller 80 bass. Then an accordion salesman came on board the ship and let me play a 120 bass that I couldn't resist, so now I had two.

I spent hours teaching myself to play. Other men heard me practicing and asked if I would teach them. It seemed like a hopeless task for some who didn't have any natural musical ability, but I gave some lessons anyway. It was something to do.

Life on board the ship during a cruise was pretty dull apart from the work. Every night an old movie was shown in our "outdoor theater." These old reel movies had lots of problems. There were interruptions while the operator figured out how to get the projector running again.

We had an occasional talent show. It was surprising to discover the talent among our crew members.

Much of my time was spent on correspondence courses. I studied courses that prepared me for advancement. The tests were quite easy for me because I had completed the courses for First Class and Chief Petty Officer before I took the test for Second Class. I registered with International Correspondence School to take the coursework for civil engineering. The first half of the course was studying material for becoming a structural engineer. The materials were set up in small study books that usually came three at a time. The mail was very slow in those days, so I spent time waiting for the next assignments.

I enjoyed the assignment that called for designing my dream house. My dream houses were small because I had never lived in a house other than the little house on our farm. To this day I'm amazed when I see what most people think they need to be comfortable. The more we have, the more we want.

Lots of men on the ship, especially on the deck force, couldn't read very well, so I spent some of my time tutoring men who asked for help. As the word got around, more men asked for help. Before long I had a little study hall filled with students. I got quite familiar with the advancement course for third class petty officer on the deck force. One of my favorite students was a first-class boatswain (bo'sn) who really wanted to be a chief petty officer but couldn't pass the test. He bought an accordion like mine, so I spent some time teaching him about the accordion as well. Unfortunately, his stubby little calloused fingers had a hard time hitting the right buttons.

I spent time every evening in the drafting room writing to my dear wife. My letters would stack up until I heard that mail would be leaving. I numbered the letters so Muriel would know which one to read first. The Bell Helicopter made a mail run about once a week to a nearby airbase in Turkey. They dropped off the out-going mail and picked up the in-coming mail. That was always an exciting event for most of the crew and a sad day for some. We reminded ourselves, "If you don't send mail, you probably won't get mail."

262

The crew suspended work while we watched for the helicopter to return with the mail. One day we were lined up along the rail when we saw the helicopter in the distance. Imagine our reaction when we saw the helicopter flying lower and lower and finally falling into the ocean! The Captain sent out a rescue crew and we managed to rescue the helicopter crew and hoist the helicopter on board. The bags of mail, and other cargo, ended up on the bottom of the ocean and never were recovered.

Some years before my time on the USS Tanner, the ship had been working near Iceland and Greenland. The Fleet Post Office dropped the mail bags on a high point to be picked up by the helicopter crew, but one bag of mail got lost in a snowstorm. When it was found years later, one of my co-workers that was serving a second time on the USS Tanner shared a letter that had been lost. It was from his dad. By the time he got the letter, his dad had been dead for two years. He shed some tears, even though he had known about his father's death for some time. He said, "This is a little spooky!"

One of my favorite volunteer jobs was setting up for worship on Sunday morning. We brought benches from the mess hall up on the foc'sle (front of the ship, top deck). We worshiped early before it got too hot, and I played the organ for worship. It was a little box organ (combat organ) that folded open and had to be pumped with foot pedals. One Easter, I decided it would be nice to have some special music and announced a "choir practice." I was surprised by the number of men who showed up. We sang three-part harmony; lead, tenor and bass. We weren't very good, but who cares? We got a nice round of applause.

A small ship called the USS Pursuit traveled with us. We always joked that the crew should receive both submarine pay and flight pay because, in a storm, they almost went under and then rode the next wave almost out of the water. On Sunday mornings, the chaplain and I rode a helicopter over to the Pursuit and dropped down with the hoist. I had to strap the little box organ to me for the descent, which must have been quite a site for the crew below. They always applauded when we came down on the cable. After the service, the chaplain and I stayed for Sunday dinner. I learned that they had better food on their ship than we did on ours. I know they had the same "stores" as we did, so it had something to do with their cook.

When we passed near a town of any size, our commissary officer would take a crew ashore on the helicopter to pick up fresh fruits and vegetables. Most of our daily rations were either canned or dried, so anything fresh was special. We had to wait for our return to home port to get fresh meat, milk, and eggs.

Our mid cruise liberty port was Istanbul. I enjoyed visiting the open bazaars where we could shop. I was a pipe smoker, so I bought a supply of meerschaum pipes. Some were carved and others were lined with meerschaum. These pipes didn't require any breaking in because the hot tobacco didn't come into contact with the wooden bowl. Other trinkets were made by Turkish craftsmen who gathered beer cans and made things to sell with them. Sometimes we could tell what kind of beer can it was made

264

of. Lots of things were made of brass. I bought a variety of candle holders which cost practically nothing. A favorite tourist item was their puzzle rings. They taught us how to solve the puzzle ring, but it wasn't long before I forgot.

As part of my liberty, I took a cruise on the Black Sea and got into a little trouble. To entertain those on the cruise, some young boys climbed up the yard arm and dove into the water. As a typical tourist, I pulled out my camera to take some pictures of the boys. We had passed into Russian territory, so Russian soldiers were on the boat. Of course, I didn't know we were in Russian territory until the soldiers took me by the arm and led me to a room on a lower deck. I thought, "Oh dear, I'm in trouble now." I was dressed in my dress whites with "USS Tanner" on my shoulder, but they didn't know what that meant. Finally, they brought out a chart with pictures of national flags. I pointed to the American flag. They brought me topside again and let me go. Before they gave my camera back, they pulled the film out and threw it in the waste basket.

Persian Gulf

My last cruise on the USS Tanner was to the Persian Gulf. When we arrived there and felt the heat, we knew we had been on vacation in the Eastern Mediterranean. On days when it was too hot to work topside, the ship cruised slowly to keep a little air moving. The evaporators on our old ship had a difficult time making fresh water from the sea water. The water we had was warm. The dry milk that was made from the water was also warm. Now that I remember those days, I really appreciate the cold water that flows freely from the faucets in our kitchen.

I don't have very clear memories of our time spent in the Persian Gulf. I just think of hot sands, hot winds, and hot steel decks. I do remember our mid-cruise visit to Karachi, Pakistan. What stands out are memories of the street people. As we walked along the sidewalks, we had to step over sick people and beggars. I felt sad and I thought to myself, "I am never going to forget this. It will help me remember to be grateful for what we have in our country." Now, as I think back to that visit, the sadness returns. I'm fascinated by the fact that my cardiologist is from that area. Many of my heart doctors are from India and Pakistan. This is perhaps an inaccurate picture, but they all seem to be thin, careful about what they eat, and dedicated to exercise. They look like they weigh about 130 pounds. The only reason I know about their life habits is that they try to convince me to eat and exercise the way they do. It's quite simple: lots of vegetables, the greener the better, raw preferred, and lots of fluids.

I spent most of this cruise in the print shop, typing on the vari-typer. Occasionally, the chief felt sorry for me and let me go to a beach camp to set up a tower. Our camps were nothing like the camps we set up in the mountains of Turkey. The one I was on was out in the desert. What I remember most was our classy toilet. It was made of wood in the carpenter shop on the ship. It was a wooden box with a hole in the top. We dug a hole in the sand and set the box over the hole. There wasn't a lot of privacy, but there were no people around except our co-workers.

One day a friendly visitor stopped by. He was riding a beautiful horse, and I'm always interested in horses. Come to think of it, I never met a horse who wasn't quite nice. This man was very handsome in his robes and turban. He spoke perfect English, and in our conversation, I learned that he was a Harvard graduate. Before he rode off into the sunset, he was kind enough to leave a bottle of authentic Jack Daniels for me and my co-workers to enjoy. We did, even without ice.

In Karachi I visited several shops where craftsmen were working with wood, making things that were inlaid with ivory or with an ivory substitute. I purchased several items that I thought Muriel would enjoy. The largest was a coffee table inlaid with an ivory substitute. They explained to us that real ivory was very expensive because elephants were scarce. Those items were available only on the black market and that was dangerous. After all this time, about sixty years, some of the inlay has fallen out, but the table still amazes me. A large serving tray, purchased about the same time, is still in vintage condition.

On Christmas Day the family of an oil executive invited ten sailors from our ship to dinner with his family. I was one of the fortunate ones to be chosen. We were dropped off at a dock, and a limo came to pick us up. The driver drove up to a gate opened by a gate keeper. We were in a beautiful gated estate made even more beautiful by a gardener. We were served our dinner in an elegant dining room with fine china, silver, and crystal. A servant poured drinks, another served food, and another was busy in the kitchen making a gourmet meal. The family was very gracious, but I felt very uneasy. In those days we controlled the resources of other nations and they were our friends. Now they have reclaimed their resources, and, in many cases, we have become the enemy.

New Year's Day my final year was special because it signaled that the time of my future discharge was approaching. I tried not to think about it because it only made the time seem to go more slowly. But, think about it I did. There were six months left of my four years, and from time to time I thought, "Maybe this is the last time I will have to do this."

For example, Shore Patrol. I never enjoyed Shore Patrol duty. That was one of the drawbacks of being a petty officer. Every time any crew members went ashore at a liberty port, the list of Shore Patrolmen was posted. If we were going to be in port for a while, we would tie up to the pier. If not, we would anchor offshore. The

268

task was to protect our crew members from getting into trouble or getting hurt. On one occasion we anchored offshore and took the liberty bound crew members ashore in one of the LCVPs. Going ashore was not the problem. Coming back with a boat full of drunks was the problem. Halfway back to the ship, one of them decided to go for a swim so he jumped overboard. We quickly stopped the boat and, while we were trying to fish him out of the water, ten more men jumped in. "Why me, Lord?" I thought as we pulled the last one back into the boat.

On another occasion, a drunk sailor started to give me a hard time while I was on Shore Patrol, calling me names and pushing me around. I never liked to write anyone up, so I put up with his antics the best I knew how - patiently. While I held my cool during the incident, I couldn't get it out of my mind. When we were back on board the ship, I checked the duty roster and noticed that he was on watch at midnight in the radio shack alone. I went to see him at his duty station to confront him about his behavior since he would have no friends around. I said, "You started a conversation with me this afternoon that we didn't finish." He knew immediately what I was referring to and fell all over himself to apologize. "Oh, I'm sorry. That was the alcohol talking. I hope you know I didn't mean anything by it." Something inside me was a little disappointed that the apology came so easily.

My last cruise finally came to an end and we headed back across the Atlantic. We traveled at our normal cruising speed, seven knots. It took us about two weeks to cross the Atlantic Ocean. That was about twice as fast as the time was passing for me as I waited for my discharge. I tried to resist the temptation to cross the days off the calendar one by one, but eventually I gave in and started the count down.

Surveyor Camp Life

Surveyors were the lucky ones who got to go ashore and live in shore camps while the rest of the crew did the work on the ship. In the evenings while we were in Turkey, we would take the Jeep down to the shore to swim in the beautiful Mediterranean water. In those days there were long stretches of white sandy beaches with very few tourists. We were accustomed to "skinny dipping." We often found old Roman coins along the coast among the remains of old castles.

At our campsites we kept an eye out for snakes. Cobras were not welcome, but they didn't need an invitation. One day we came back from work to find one in our tent. None of us knew exactly what to do, but our onion woman showed up at just the right time. (We were happy to buy onions from her to make our canned rations taste better.) On this occasion, she was our hero. She rescued us by catching the cobra and carrying it off. She was amazing.

On the beaches near the larger towns and cities were open-air restaurants. A platter of shish kebob with rice cost thirty-five cents. The cab drivers were all very happy to exchange our dollars for lira at an amazing rate. The cabbies paid us four or five times as much as we could get from the official exchange stations (black market). The Turks also liked American cigarettes of any kind and paid a good price for them.

I had a shipmate who was a French Canadian from northern Maine. Leon got along very well in Turkey because he looked like one of them. I wasn't so fortunate. I looked like any other American. Leon was a mountain man and talked often about hunting and trapping. He had a matched pair of 356 Magnum pistols that he stored in the ship's armory. He bragged that these pistols were powerful enough to bring down a bear. Occasionally he brought them out, took them apart, oiled them up, and put them back. I guess he needed to admire them from time to time. Leon didn't drink a drop of liquor and never smoked a cigarette. However, he seldom left the ship without a supply of cigarettes to barter with.

On one occasion when we were working near Israel, the officer and chief petty officer who were with us on that task force had worn their uniforms while we "blue collar" sailors were dressed in dungarees. We were not allowed to travel in Israel without our dress uniforms, so we never got to be tourists. The "upper-class sailors" came back from their excursion full of reports of what we were missing.

The trip I enjoyed most was our assignment to make new maps of the area around the Bahamas. We didn't know until later that we were making new ocean charts in preparation for the start of the space program. Our camp sites were on the beautiful beaches of the Caribbean. Our work centered around Grand Bahama

Island, and at the end of each workday we had time to swim in the clear blue water. We gathered conch shells, and the locals taught us how to eat conch. They cautioned us because some were edible and others were not. The shells were beautiful.

Small boys came to our campsite and were curious about our work. They amazed us by their ability to climb the coconut palm trees. They could climb like monkeys, and they knocked down coconuts for us to enjoy. They taught us about drinking the coconut water and eating the raw coconut meat. We taught ourselves to add rum to the coconut water to make a delicious mixed drink.

Some of the islands had small villages, and the people all seemed to have beautiful voices. I heard them singing and realized they knew quite a few gospel songs. I got permission to bring the combat organ ashore and, since I played by ear, I could easily identify the key they were singing in and play along. They seemed to love to sing with accompaniment. I hope they enjoyed making music with me as much as I did with them.

Enjoying Grandchildren

This story started with my discharge from the US Navy and the purchase of my canoe. My canoe is somewhat battered from nearly sixty years of use on lakes and rivers. Most of the dents have come from river rapids where the canoe banged into rocks along the way down river.

The idea of retirement didn't appeal to me. Finally, at age 80, I decided it was time. I have retired from serving congregations to life at our cabin on Horseshoe Lake, and my canoe has retired from the rugged life on river trips to quiet early rides on a still morning. It is a faithful companion that lies quietly on the beach, waiting patiently for me.

Many people comment that they seem to be busier in retirement than they were when they were working. The same is true for me. However, there is a significant difference. When I'm not working for a paycheck I find it easier to say, "Not today." There are few real obligations and more choices. So, while I'm still quite busy, my time is my own. That's a special kind of freedom.

Much of the time I reflect about my children and grandchildren. They are the blessings in my life that top my many other blessings. I talk so often about my children, many of my friends know their names even though they have never met them.

Arlene and Jim, our special friends, always asked about the children. When our grandchildren were born, Arlene wrote a special poem for each of the first four. Unfortunately, she suffered from diabetes and died before she got to know the rest.

Matt and Monica have two children, Kyle and Leah. These are the poems she wrote when they were born:

On the birth of Kyle

You sing in our minds of your father's life,
But with heart chords all of your own.

You dance in our visions, we laugh with your joy.
You cry, and we hold you tight.

You find in our hearts a garden walled,
A safe place for people to grow.

We tenderly nurture the seed as it sprouts,
And celebrate sunshine and rain.

We stand in the shadows our care always near,
And marvel as your life unfolds.

The story is old but it never repeats,
Your life is a gift of its own.

Kyle is now at Hendrix College in Arkansas. He is tall and handsome with a gentle disposition. Kyle plays the bass guitar. My 80th birthday was made more special when he played with me for a Christmas sing-along with the family.

Kyle

On the birth of Leah

First there was just your father
Then he brought us a daughter to love
Together they gave us your brother
Now you've joined our circle of love.

You have so much to experience
To feel, to see, and to know,
We saved a big place in the circle
So you'll have plenty of room to grow.

There's room for your wobbly first steps
And your confident striding through life.
Room for your giggling laughter
And your soul-stirring quest for light.

There's room for your years of growing
For questions, daydreams and play
There's room in our love for tomorrow
As we cuddle you closely today.

Leah

Leah is now preparing for graduation from high school and busy choosing a college for her next life adventure. She loves drama. I have enjoyed watching her perform several times in the

Nutcracker. This year she did an amazing performance with the church youth group in the play, "High School Prom."

Nancy and Charles have two children, Vanessa and Charlie. These are the poems Arlene wrote at the time of their births:

On the birth of Vanessa

O child of my child
How will it be?
Will you teach me of wonder again?

Shall I blow on your toes or comfort small woes
And cuddle you close to my heart?
You act as a lens and focus the time,
Long ago, yet yesterday,
When your mother was new and helpless like you,
While her future was daydreams and play.

O child of my child,
Who will you be?
Your mother, your father, and more?

Will you store up the joys as you play with your toys
To strengthen a lifetime of light?

Will you doubt in the shadows, yet see yourself clearly,
A wondrous gift from above?

Content with the claim of a link in that chain
The continuing heirloom of love.

Vanessa

Vanessa has graduated from Denison University with a degree in Psychology and is now working as an admissions counselor at Purdue University in Indiana. She also minored in music and has had a wonderful singing career in her young life. She sang several years in the Columbus Children's Choir and did two European tours with the group.

On the birth of Charlie

O tiny child,
How can those hands
So tightly hold our hearts?

Thoughts disappear while senses fill
(What magic in this art?)
Our fingers feel your velvet skin,
Your sleepy sigh still charms,
Your rounded form, the weight of you,
Still snuggles in our arms

O tiny child,
Tomorrow comes with diary unmarred,
We look ahead to baseball games,
To butterflies and stars;

To questions without answers,
To wisdom grown through tears,
To a celebration of your life
That lasts through all our years.

Charlie loves sports. He played baseball and football during his young life, until he graduated from Pickerington Central High School. Now he is a student at the University of Miami in Florida studying criminal justice. Recently he was fortunate to have an opportunity to do an internship with a judge in Columbus, Ohio.

Charlie

When I married Ruth, in 2009, I was blessed with three new grandchildren. At that time, Tom and Livia lived in Budapest, Hungary. They have three wonderful, talented children - Thomas, Balint and Aliz.

I've never forgotten their first visit to our home on the lake. The boys were interested in what I was doing and eager to help. I was putting the finishing touches on our new kitchen cabinets. Thomas and Balint loved to hand me whatever I needed next - a tool, a knob, or a nut. I was amazed how quickly they knew what to do. Now that I know them, I should not have been amazed because each is brilliant in his own way.

Thomas is a typical first child. He is dependable and helpful. He loves to work with his hands. Now a junior in high school, he is a runner on the cross-country team, a good student, and recently exploring the field of drama.

Balint, a freshman in high school, is a musician. When Ruth brought one of our violins to Hungary, as a small child he claimed it as his own. As the years have flown by, he proved that he meant it. He practices with amazing discipline and plays in a community orchestra. He is also an excellent student, seldom satisfied with less than perfection.

Aliz, a fifth grader, is small but mighty. She attacks life with gusto and does her best to keep up with her big brothers. She dances, swims, and most recently plays volleyball. One of my favorite memories of our visit to Hungary is a day in the forest. In Hungary, many families go for walks along the forest paths on Sunday afternoon. It is a wonderful custom. As we walked, Aliz could not allow herself to get behind. She ran ahead to be the leader. But, from time to time, she had to take a detour to explore something she saw off the beaten path.

Our three children from Ethiopia each have brought two grandchildren into our family circle.

Dawit and Shannon had a daughter, Laensa. She is a brilliant student and a gifted athlete. As a young girl she loved soccer and was a very good soccer player. I remember a day when we were visiting her family in Denver. I asked, "How did your soccer game go?"

Laensa said, "Fine."

"Did you win?" I asked.

"Yes," she replied

"What was the score?"

"Three to nothing," she replied.

"Did you score?" I asked.

"Three times," she said with a smile.

Laensa graduated early from high school and is now studying at the University of Vermont.

Dawit and his wife, Zena, have a young child named Hasset. We are getting to know her primarily through pictures. As I write, I'm looking at her picture. She is a honey.

Wengel also has two children. Adina is tiny but very intelligent. Precocious is the word for her. We have to be content with pictures to keep up with the growth of Adina and her brother Yonatan. He, too, is very intelligent.

Some time ago we went to Denver to visit. We were seated in the living room, listening as the two small children played. Adina was playing house with her girl toys, and Yonatan was playing nearby with his construction toys. Their conversation sounded like adults talking in children's voices. I don't remember what Adina shared with him, but Yonatan responded, "That is astonishing."

Banti and Nicole have two daughters, Helena and Liliana. They are delightful little girls. Once again, we rely on pictures to keep up to date with them. It sounds like a broken record, but they too are very good students.

That completes the story of our thirteen grandchildren. Many colors, many nationalities, many blessings.

Preoccupied with Prisons and Prisoners

Now that I am free from ministry in congregations, I am able to devote more time to ex-prisoners, prisoners, and prisons. My involvement with them is as a counselor, an AA sponsor, or just an old friend.

I seldom go anywhere without meeting someone who remembers me, usually with fondness. How blessed I am. At a program presented by refugees a few evenings ago, I was waiting to meet one of the refugees who I had sponsored many years ago. While I waited in a corner of the lobby, several ex-prisoner friends took turns waiting to talk to me. These men were obviously successful in their lives after prison. Each one's story is different.

Erik had been in and out of prison three times as he struggled with drug addiction. I hadn't seen him for at least ten years. In the meantime, he had successfully kicked his habit, had gained full custody of his three daughters, had raised them through high school, and had finished his own bachelor's degree. He heaped praise on me for all that I did for him, but the praise belongs to him and our Higher Power for what he has done for himself and his children. To God be the glory.

288

Some stories do not have a happy ending, but that is true for people who have never been in prison as well. Marty stopped by our house last week with his wife and two of his four children. Together we recalled their wedding ten years ago. It took place in front of my Christmas tree at the cabin. Marty and Kim had been a couple before he went to prison. They had two children and, when he was released from prison twelve years ago, they decided to get married. Since then they have had a good life and have had two more children. Recently they learned that Marty has stage four cancer and treatment has done all that it can for him. They talked openly in front of the two children about his impending death. In spite of the sadness, they seemed like a healthy family and I was proud of them. Pastors know what an honor it is to share such intimate stories, even sad stories, with people who trust us.

Lee was a prisoner twenty years ago. He was very active in Followers of Christ Church in the Nebraska State Penitentiary. We talked at least once a week, and Lee was determined he would be successful when released. We helped him with some work clothes, an apartment, furnishings for the apartment, and a temporary job. Alcohol almost destroyed him, however. He was willing to work hard, but often I came to his apartment and found him drunk or drinking. I implored him to go to treatment, but he was not interested. He had a seven-year-old daughter and was determined to be reunited with her. After he got permission from her foster mother to see her, he learned that his daughter had brain cancer. We attended her funeral together, but that fueled the drinking even more. He had construction skills, especially in electrical wiring. I hired him to wire my new shop and garden shed. The inspector complimented him, saying, "I haven't seen such good work for many years. With quality work like this, I won't need to return for a final inspection." Lee was proud. I was proud. But the drinking went on.

Lee got a job doing some work for a lady who owned rental properties in Lincoln. She, too, was very impressed by the quality of his work. She hired him to take care of her property. He was proud that she trusted him with all the keys. He advertised, "Lee's Home Improvement," and got lots of other calls as well. But the drinking went on.

One night, Lee met Sandy at a bar. They started dating and soon were living together. Lee was functioning as Dad for Sandy's two children. He was a good dad, but the drinking went on.

Finally, the drinking took its toll on Lee's kidneys and he was in great pain. Sandy and I took him to the hospital, and from there to detox. He finally agreed to treatment. He saw the light. Now his health is restored, he has reunited with his birth family and married Sandy. They have raised her children together and are caring for his mother in their home.

A couple of weeks ago I was sitting in a fast food restaurant waiting to meet another man who just started his life on the outside and I saw Lee in line to pick up takeout food. The restaurant was full of construction workers on their lunch break. Lee turned around, saw me, and shouted, "Pastor Bud!" and rushed to my table. What a joy!

290

And then there is a my very special friend, Chuck. I met Chuck at a Freed for LIFE Dinner. He was one of the speakers, telling his story. I watched when the program was over as people gathered around to tell him how impressed they were with his speaking ability. I was one of the crowd. That was the beginning of a relationship that has gone from AA sponsor, to counselor, to good friend, to "the Dad he never had. "

Chuck has struggled with alcohol. When we met, neither he nor I were very fond of AA meetings. Together we learned that AA has much to offer people like us. We started attending meetings together, and he now is approaching four years sobriety. He has reunited with his three daughters and his five grandchildren. He is a very hard worker in the construction field. He bought a duplex and completely remodeled it. He loves gardening and raises garden produce to share with anyone and everyone he meets.

Recently, Chuck met Rosanne through an online dating service. Roseanne is a blessing for Chuck. Together they are a blessing for Ruth and me. Chuck comes nearly every week to mow our lawn and make miscellaneous repairs at our home. He always comes with a tool or two in his pocket. "Mama Ruth," as he calls her, has learned to love him as much as I do.

The stories in my memory go on and on. Perhaps these few stories will reveal how blessed I am to be doing the work that I do. To God be the glory!

What If?

In retirement I have time at the lake, especially on my morning canoe rides, to pray and to dream about what could be. Recently I have been revisiting some old dreams. I wonder to myself, and sometimes with other listeners, whether some components of my dreams might still come true.

During my daily visits to the prison, I always felt sad that so many men with strong bodies and good minds were wasting their days. I spent a lot time listening to their stories, their hopes, and their dreams.

When the day finally came for someone's sentence to end or for their parole to begin, I met them at the gate and we started the walk together into their new future. For many of them, the way forward was too steep a climb and they ended up back behind bars. One hundred dollars gate pay did not last long when they had no place to live, no food to eat, no transportation, and no appropriate clothing.

I often think of my own alcohol rehabilitation experience, and I realize that the most useful part of that experience came through education. After a couple of years of hard work, I ended up with a Doctor of Education Degree. I was not the same person I had been before. But I had the support of a wonderful wife and family through those long, hard days.

I wish that lots of prisoners could have a similar experience instead of sitting, waiting, and wasting time that could be used productively if it were allowed. A few of them get their GED and a few are able to take some correspondence courses if they have support from their families. That led me to dream about what we, the public, might do for these valuable people who are totally dependent on us. As my wife, Muriel, said so often, "These people are our brothers, our sisters, somebody's children, and in some cases our fathers, mothers and grandfathers/grandmothers. If we help them, we also help those who love them."

I saw a few lucky prisoners going to work in the shops. I wondered what it would be like if we could develop partnerships between the prison and the community so many more men and women could do productive work.

As I travel around to speak and raise money to help prisoners, I meet many people who are hostile toward prisoners and my ideas to help them.

"They deserve what they got!"

"Put them behind bars and throw away the key."

"I don't want them in my neighborhood or my community."

I have always had an interest in recycling. I have read about recycling programs that are developing in other states and other nations and wondered, why not here in Nebraska? What if we developed a recycling program in our state that put prisoners to work saving our landfills and even our planet? What if these recycling programs produced by-products that had real value, turning garbage into compost, fertilizer, methane gas, or mulch?

Businesspeople in our communities raise the question of "unfair competition" from workshops in the prison because prisoners are forced to work for such small wages. What if we developed more work sites in the prison and paid the prisoners real wages? Then they could pay taxes, pay their child support, and we could put some of their earnings into an education account to help them pay for tuition and books.

What if we required every prisoner to put in a full day of work, study, or some of each?

What if prisoners were leaving prison with good skills and/or academic degrees?

What if our parole officers and probation officers were trained as "life coaches" to help parolees solve real problems in their lives on the outside?

What if we built homes inside the prison and taught building skills to prisoners, and then let those on work release finish the job on the outside?

What if we would partner with agencies like Habitat for Humanity?

What if we would partner with educational institutions to offer coursework inside the prisons? Perhaps prisoners could earn the right to "study release." Perhaps each correction center could have a unit for those who have earned the right to work release and/or study release.

What if research institutions would study good things that are happening in prisons around the nation and around the world and could feed valuable information to us as we build our programs? Perhaps "think tanks" could keep processing and dreaming, and talented entrepreneurs could help put dreams into action.

We are spending huge amounts of money to warehouse prisoners, and we complain about the high cost of operating prisons. But the alternatives to warehousing are real!

In my experience, most progress begins with a dream, or a dreaming process. Scripture says, "Old men shall dream dreams...." That's me, still dreaming.

Currently, I'm dreaming about a truck driving school for prisoners. I'm also exploring the possibility of organic farming (gardening) on some of the available land at our prisons. Please join me in praying for our prisoners and our prisons.

The Flood

I have lived in my cabin home for twenty-two years. Only once, in 2011, was I threatened by a flood. Fortunately, it never reached my house. The representatives from the county sheriff's office came and told me I had to leave immediately. I left, but I knew I would be back in a day or two, so I took just a few things with me. The flood waters started to recede the next day and I was back at home.

This year (2019), on a Thursday morning, the representatives from the county sheriff's office came around again. They knocked on our door and told us we must leave immediately. Once again, Ruth and I left as ordered, and took with us clothes for only two days. We went to Elkhorn to stay with my daughter Julie and her husband, Jason, but believed we would be back at home in a couple of days. This time, however, Mother Nature surprised us. The flood waters kept rising.

Our dear friend, Chuck, rushed out to our place and called to say he would break the bathroom window and save what he could from the murky flood waters. He knew Ruth wanted that window replaced anyway. He knew us well and knew what we treasured most. He carried my grandfather clock up to my shop, carried our recliners to a safe place, and he and Jason put Ruth's beautiful piano up on blocks.

While the waters were still rising, Julie and several of her friends rushed out to the lake and packed up everything in our house and moved it to higher ground in the shop.

While all of this was happening, we were safe and warm at Julie and Jason's house enjoying Tulip and Dauby, their dogs. The inevitable question surfaced, "What do we do now?" We had shared thoughts about leaving the lake someday, but each time we set those thoughts aside for a later conversation.

We thought about how difficult it was for me to care for the lawn and the beach. Chuck came out to do our yard work in the summer and shovel the snow in the winter. We thought about how difficult it was for us to navigate the icy slope that led to where we parked our cars.

It became obvious to us that this was the opportune time for us to make a move. The thought about leaving our lake home had been too difficult for me to contemplate. Now, it could no longer be avoided.

There was an amazing amount of work ahead to make our cabin home livable again. The smelly flood waters permeated the walls, the kitchen cabinets, the furniture, and the appliances. There were public warnings to beware of dangers that lurked in the flood waters, such as E. coli.

We moved very quickly to report our flood damage to our flood insurance. In a day or two we had a visit from a FEMA assessor. Our daughter, Julie, took pictures of everything and prepared a spreadsheet of restoration work as it was being done. Our son-in-law, Jason, stepped up and took over the restoration process. With the help of some volunteers, he cleaned up the mud, removed insulation and damaged walls inside and out, tore out the bottom kitchen cabinets, and sent all the damaged items to the dump. Then he put together a plan to rebuild the house. When all of this was finished, someone would have a new home.

One day, Senator Sasse, his family, and some friends came by to help with the clean-up process. That was a pleasant surprise.

In a couple of weeks, we received an advance payment from FEMA. That helped us move forward with the purchase of supplies and new kitchen cabinets.

We are blessed to have a wonderful family who can do what Ruth and I could never do by ourselves. Most of our family offers encouragement from a distance. Julie and Jason have done, and are doing, an amazing amount of organizing and lots of just plain hard work from up close.

We looked online for senior independent living options. We identified two that interested us but learned that only one option had apartments available. Carriage Glen had three available apartments with rent that was within our price range, so we made a visit. It turned out to be the perfect place for this new phase of our life. We had made a list of what we wanted, and it provided everything we needed, particularly the underground parking for both cars. We both liked it and made the decision on the spot to make this our new home. We moved our beds and a few items of furniture, moved our clothes into the closet, and slept the first night in our new bedroom.

Now we are faced with all the things our daughter and her friends stuffed into totes and carried to my shop. Downsizing is not easy, but it was necessary for us. We have to make decisions about what is important enough to keep, what our kids would like to have, what to throw away, and what is worth giving away.

We daily remind each other that we are very fortunate. We hear story after story of flood victims who have absolutely nothing left. Some have lost their cars and trucks. Our cars are parked safely in our underground private parking spaces. Some people lost all of their furniture. We lost some of our furniture but have plenty left to fill our new apartment. The beat goes on. We are blessed!

Thank You

From time to time I revisit the twelve steps in the AA program. The steps have been a blessing to me. They are not easy.

1. We admitted we were powerless over alcohol—that our lives had *become unmanageable.*
2. Came to believe that a Power greater than ourselves could restore us to sanity.
3. Made a decision to turn our will and our lives over to the care of God as we understood him.
4. Made a searching and fearless moral inventory of ourselves.
5. Admitted to God, to ourselves, and to another human being the exact nature of our wrongs.
6. Were entirely ready to have God remove all these defects of *character.*
7. Humbly asked Him to remove our shortcomings.
8. Made a list of all persons we had harmed, and became willing to make amends to them all.
9. Made direct amends to such people wherever possible, except when to do so would injure them or others.

10. Continued to take personal inventory and when we were wrong promptly admitted it.

11. Sought through prayer and meditation to improve our conscious contact with God as we understood Him, praying only for knowledge of His will for us and the power to carry that out.

12. Having had a spiritual awakening as the result of these steps, we tried to carry this message to alcoholics, and to practice these *principles in all our affairs.*

(From the fourth edition of The Big Book, Alcoholics Anonymous.)

Steps eight and nine are especially important to me. My attempts to share my apology and to make amends have met with mixed results. Some people seem to be embarrassed for me and shove my apology aside.

Some say, "Oh, you're not an alcoholic." Some of my friends don't want to admit that I'm an alcoholic because it shines the light on their own struggles.

After my latest bout with alcohol, I seemed to be more successful with steps eight and nine. People I spoke to seemed more receptive. That was true of my children as well. Perhaps it's because I have gotten better at talking about it.

Now I have initiated a new practice. I have made a list of people who have been good to me or helpful to me in my life. I am taking these people out to lunch to say thank you. That has been a blessing for me. It makes me happy to see the surprised look on their faces. For me, it is like looking forward to Christmas. Each time I say thank you to someone, I enjoy the anticipation of our time together for several days in advance.

Some of my friends are too far away to get together for lunch. I enjoy writing thank you letters to them. Some of them answer my letter and some of them don't. I know we live in a world where snail mail seems to be a nuisance, but I haven't learned to appreciate e-mail and texting. I'm not adept at using my computer or texting on my phone. My kids think my little old phone is part of the problem. It doesn't seem like on old phone to me. It doesn't have a rotary dial or a party line.

I enjoy receiving a thank you as much as giving one. I have been browsing through some keepsake mail recently and decided to include some thank you letters that I have received. This is a copy of one that was sent to our Bishop Richard Jessen with a copy to me.

Dear Bishop Jessen:

Our Senior High youth had the privilege of worshipping with the members of Followers of Christ Lutheran Church and Pastor Bud Christenson on Saturday, February 26th. What a marvelous opportunity to see God at work. I can honestly say that none of us who attended that worship service will ever be the same. The impact as you know, is life-changing.

After worship all of us spent time over dinner processing what we had seen, heard and felt. I asked the youth and adults to please write a simple essay reflecting their experience. I am enclosing two of these essays. One youth essay and one essay written by one of our adults. They are both very powerful and a real testimony to the importance of this ministry for the inmates, for those of us who have the opportunity to visit, and for our church as a whole.

Thank you so much for your encouragement, support and affirmation of this opportunity to serve so many different people. It is a blessing for so many. Our young people and adults are anxious to return to this place of hope and love. Our Senior High youth have even asked the Church Council for permission to send their Sunday school offering monies to Pastor Christenson for prison ministry. The high school offering last Sunday was $29.00. What a difference connecting to others makes!

Again, all that you do for all of us is greatly appreciated but seldom said.

In Christ,
Sheryl Griess AIM
Rejoice Lutheran Church, Omaha

Youth Essay

My Prison Worship Experience:

"For God so loved the world that he gave his only son...." His only son to die for us on a cross, so that we may have eternal life. So that we may have eternal life? All law-abiding citizens, all Christians, all never-miss-a-Sunday church goers? How could God possibly send his son to die on a cross for people who would murder and steal from their fellow man? How could God's love and mercy ever penetrate these prison walls?

These questions baffled me, but what really struck fear into my heart, was going to this prison, and finding no God at all. Going into this place of despair and loneliness, and finding no hope and comfort. What would this say about me, about my sins, about my God? How far can one stray from this narrow road, before God stops loving you? How big a sin is unforgivable?

I need not fear though. I had only to step into the small auditorium converted to a sanctuary, sing just one hymn, and watch with amazement at the friendliness of the prisoners. There was something in these souls, something only God could give. You saw it as they stood and clapped after Chuck sang Merciful God. So sincerely touched were they that it made my heart swell with a love I had never felt before. Love for these criminals, these sinful human beings who I was always taught to fear and never thought I had the capacity to love. God was there. You could see it in Pastor Bud's eyes, you could hear it in his voice. The love he had for these men, and the love they had for him. And in this place of despair and lost hope, you could see God's love. You could feel it. My heart leapt with joy, if God's mercy could touch these men, then he could touch me. If God's love could travel to the depths of the darkened human spirit, then it could travel anywhere.

And as I left the prison, I was finally able to fully understand what that Bible verse really means. God sent his son to die for all of his children, the good and the bad, the righteous and the unrighteous. Christ died for all sinners and God's promise of salvation belongs to us all, even the men behind these prison walls.

Julie Gunderson

This thank you came from the president of Wartburg Theological Seminary, Dubuque, Iowa.

Dr. M. L. Christenson
17600 Fedde Lane
Ashland, NE 68003

Dear Bud:

With the last boxes unpacked in Colorado, there has been time to reflect again on the events of early November in Dubuque. The program for the "celebration, recognition and thanksgiving" event is on our coffee table and the two large pictures of Wartburg Seminary grace our walls—one in the living room and the Chapel one next to my desk. We've had occasion to play the video for our own reflection and with our mothers, who were not able to attend the event.

Marilyn and I want to thank you for your part in that memorable evening. We thank you for your reflections, reaching back to our life together in the Central District and forward into the years during which you have been a member of this board. You remember some things I had long forgotten. Thank you! Special thanks for your outstanding service as chairman of the board for these past six years. You have helped us manage through difficult and complicated times. You have been part chair and pastor to me and to the board. Thank you! Your contribution to that event was a true gift!

If travel brings you in the direction of Rocky Mountain Park, come and see us. Just give us a call.

POWER TO YOU!
Roger and Marilyn

As I come to the end of my reflections on my life, my heart is filled with thanksgiving.

Thanksgiving for a lifetime filled with blessings
The gift of the Savior. "I can do all through Christ…"
The privilege of serving God and God's church all these years
Challenges, and inspiration and strength to meet them
Loving partners to share life with
A family of wonderful children and grandchildren
A growing number of friends
The serenity that surrounds us at Horseshoe Lake
My most treasured possession, my canoe
The gift of music
Doctors who do by-passes and pacemakers

* * *

"For life, for health, for every good we give You thanks, O Lord."

* * *

Benedictions Passed on from Others

May you always walk in sunshine, slumber warm when night winds blow,
May you always live with laughter, for a smile becomes you so.
May good fortune find your doorway, may the bluebird sing your song.
May no trouble travel your way, may no worry stay too long.

May your heartaches be forgotten, may no tears be spilled,
May old acquaintance be remembered, and your cup of kindness filled.
And may you always be a dreamer, may your wildest dreams come true.
May you always love each other as much as God loves you.

* * *

"As you go on your way, may Christ go with you,
May he go before you to show you the way;
May he go behind you to encourage you;
Beside you to befriend you;
Above you to watch over you;
Within you to give you peace.
(Both may be known as Irish Blessings.)

Our Family Table Prayer

Come Lord Jesus, be our guest
Let these gifts to us be blessed. Amen.

"A Favorite Prayer"

(Prayer of St. Francis)

Lord, make me an instrument of Your peace.

Where there is hatred, let me sow love.

Where there is injury, pardon.

Where there is doubt, faith.

Where there is despair, hope.

Where there is darkness, light.

Where there is sadness, joy.

O Divine Master;

Grant that I may not so much seek to be consoled as to console;

To be understood as to understand;

To be loved as to love;

For it is in giving that we receive,

It is in pardoning that we are pardoned,

And it is in dying that we are born to eternal life.

Made in the USA
Coppell, TX
14 September 2020

37444094R00189